Going Against the Stream

Going Against the Stream

My Conversation with Bonhoeffer from Beginning to End

JOHN W. DE GRUCHY

CASCADE *Books* • Eugene, Oregon

GOING AGAINST THE STREAM
My Conversation with Bonhoeffer from Beginning to End

Copyright © 2025 John W. de Gruchy. All rights reserved. Except for brief quotations in critical publications or reviews, no part of this book may be reproduced in any manner without prior written permission from the publisher. Write: Permissions, Wipf and Stock Publishers, 199 W. 8th Ave., Suite 3, Eugene, OR 97401.

Cascade Books
An Imprint of Wipf and Stock Publishers
199 W. 8th Ave., Suite 3
Eugene, OR 97401

www.wipfandstock.com

PAPERBACK ISBN: 979-8-3852-6120-8
HARDCOVER ISBN: 979-8-3852-6121-5
EBOOK ISBN: 979-8-3852-6122-2

Cataloging-in-Publication data:

Names: De Gruchy, John W., author.

Title: Going against the stream : my conversation with Bonhoeffer from beginning to end / John W. de Gruchy.

Description: Eugene, OR: Cascade Books, 2025. | Includes bibliographical references and indexes.

Identifiers: ISBN: 979-8-3852-6120-8 (paperback). | ISBN: 979-8-3852-6121-5 (hardcover). | ISBN: 979-8-3852-6122-2 (ebook).

Subjects: LCSH: Bonhoeffer, Dietrich, 1906–1945. | Bonhoeffer, Dietrich, 1906–1945—Imprisonment. | Bonhoeffer, Dietrich, 1906–1945—Criticism and interpretation. | De Gruchy, John W. | South Africa—Race relations. | Race relations—Christianity. | Theological anthropology—Christianity. | Artificial intelligence.

Classification: BX4827.B57 D39 2025 (print). | BX4827 (epub).

Scripture quotations are taken from the New Revised Standard Version Bible © 1989 Division of Christian Education of the National Council of the Churches of Christ in the United States of America. Used by permission. All rights reserved worldwide.

In Celebration of the
Eightieth Anniversary of the Martyrdom of
Dietrich Bonhoeffer
and in Memory
of
Eberhard and Renate Bethge

In Memory of
Steve
(1961–2010)
&
In Gratitude to
Isobel
and the next generations
Jeanelle, Anton, Marian, Esther & Debra
Thea, David, Kate & George

&
in Praise of Friendship
to
Judy and Julian Cooke (1940–2025)

Contents

Preface | ix
Abbreviations | xiii

    Prologue | 1
1 Dissent in Christendom | 4
2 Happiness in a World at War | 37
3 Being Human in a Robotic World | 57
    Epilogue | 83

Bibliography | 89
Index of Names | 105
Index of Subjects | 107
Index of Scripture | 115

Preface

I HAVE BEEN IN conversation with Dietrich Bonhoeffer for more than sixty years. *Going Against the Stream* brings this conversation to a conclusion with the prayer that the reader will be as inspired and challenged by Bonhoeffer's legacy as I have been.[1] At the heart of that legacy is Bonhoeffer's witness to Christ by "going against the stream" for the sake of the life of the world. Tempting and popular as it may be to go with the cultural flow, even when it is dragging us into dangerous whirlpools, we learn from salmon that the future of life depends on struggling against the current. For this reason, Karl Barth, Bonhoeffer's mentor, used this metaphor to describe his own theology, and I in turn apply it to Bonhoeffer's.[2]

We live at a time of global crisis in which we are invited to listen afresh to the good news of Jesus Christ and seize this moment to follow him.[3] If we do, we often discover that we have embarked on a journey on which we have to learn to live by faith in order to discover life in its fullness and contribute to the common good. The journey consciously begins, as Bonhoeffer discovered, when

---

1. I have referenced my books on Bonhoeffer in these footnotes. The first was de Gruchy, *Bonhoeffer and South Africa*; and the most recent are de Gruchy, *Bonhoeffer's Questions*; and de Gruchy, *Faith Facing Reality*. See also de Gruchy, *Theological Odyssey*, 52–70.

2. Smith, Editor's Foreword, 10–11.

3. See Cullmann, *Christ and Time*, 39. Several Greek words are used in the New Testament to express time, among them *chronos* or chronological time, *aion*, a period or "age," and *kairos*, a critical moment. Their precise meaning depends on the context in which they are used. See Barr, *Biblical Words for Time*.

PREFACE

we respond to Jesus's invitation to follow him: "the time (*kairos*) is fulfilled, and the kingdom of God has come near, repent [*metanoia*, literally "change your mind"] and believe in the good news."[4]

Being a Christian, Bonhoeffer tells us, is not about becoming more religious but about allowing ourselves "to be pulled into walking the path that Jesus walks."[5] Whether we are willing to walk that path is our choice, though looking back something tells me that I could have done no other. But given the perils facing us as we are being dragged downstream toward dangerous rapids, what Christ offers by way of saving hope is surely worth considering. But there is a price tag attached to discipleship, as Bonhoeffer well knew.[6] He also discovered that when Christ becomes the foundation of our lives, we begin to experience life in all its fullness. The gospel offers us freedom, inspires creativity, and fosters deep friendships, and while it demands solidarity and empathy with those who suffer, it also keeps us happy in difficult times. Unlike the nihilism that characterizes much modern culture and finds depressing expression in dystopian movies and novels, the gospel is good news that helps us face the threatening realities of the times in which we live. So, as the writer of the Letter to the Hebrews put it, "Today, if you will hear God's voice, harden not your hearts."[7]

On January 13, 1943, while the Second World War continued to rage and to grow in intensity, Bonhoeffer became engaged to the vivacious, and much younger, Maria von Wedemeyer. At the same time, he was becoming more deeply involved in a plot to assassinate Adolf Hitler. Then, a few months later, on April 5, he was arrested by the Gestapo, not because they had knowledge of the plot, but because they suspected he was involved in helping Jews escape Germany. As a prisoner "awaiting trial" in Tegel Military Prison in Berlin, Bonhoeffer spent anxious months waiting for the frequently postponed trial to reach its verdict. Patience was not one of his virtues. Isolated in his cell, he contemplated suicide. He

---

4. Mark 1:14.
5. Bonhoeffer, *Letters and Papers*, 480.
6. See Bonhoeffer, *Discipleship*.
7. Hebrews 3:15.

also thought about writing "a small study on the 'sense of time'" to help him cope.[8] If before his imprisonment he knew how to seize the moment and act, in prison he had to learn patience and how to make the most of its boring passing. With this in mind, he jotted down some notes which I have used in writing the prologue and epilogue that sandwich the three chapters that follow.

Bonhoeffer seized the moment to go against the stream when during the Third Reich he challenged the Nazification of the Protestant Church, worked tirelessly for peace, sided with the oppressed, taught his students in an underground seminary, traveled widely, and preached often—and then, when he was banned, he joined the German Resistance. This hectic narrative informs my discussion in chapter 1, where I weave my own journey into the framework and narrative of Christian Dissent and tell how and why my conversation with Bonhoeffer began during the church struggle against apartheid.[9] In the first, chapter 2, I consider the significance of his passing comment on being happy in a time of war. What did Bonhoeffer mean by this as he began to anticipate the increasing likelihood of his own death, and what could it mean for us in these war-weary times? Should we resist fate and wear ourselves out through fretting and complaining, or patiently discern and submit to God's will? To live by faith, Bonhoeffer decided, requires "a more flexible . . . way of acting" if we are to "endure our present situation and make the most of it."[10] And making the most of it is what he did as he considered the future of Christianity in a "world come of age," briefly calling for the recovery of "aesthetic existence" in the life of the church as a "sphere of freedom." Finally, in chapter 3, I reflect on Bonhoeffer's comments on science and technology in his *Ethics* and letters from prison as I respond to the urgent question now facing us: How are

8. Bonhoeffer, *Letters and Papers*, 79.

9. See de Gruchy, *I Have Come a Long Way*, 58 et al. Earlier versions of chapters 1 and 2 were published in the *Stellenbosch Theological Journal* (*STJ*), as "Ecumenical Dissent from Christendom to Christian Nationalism," and "Christ under the Rubble: Bonhoeffer and Aesthetic Existence as a Sphere of Freedom in a Time of War."

10. Bonhoeffer, *Letters and Papers*, 303–4. The German title of *Letters and Papers* is *Widerstand und Ergebung*, that is, "Resistance and Submission."

PREFACE

we to save our souls in a world controlled by artificial general intelligence? Bonhoeffer may not have said the last word on theology in his own time, but he often did say a penultimate word that helps us respond to the issues that now confront us.

During the past twenty-three years, since I retired from the University of Cape Town, Isobel and I have been members of the Volmoed Community, established in 1986 as a center for healing and reconciliation. Located near Hermanus in the Western Cape, Volmoed is distinguished by the Onrus River flowing through to the Indian Ocean, and these magnificent surroundings have been an ideal place to write, and for Isobel to paint, write poetry, and document the Fynbos-rich floral kingdom on all sides of us. But she has also supported my writing and now, once again, examined the text with her accustomed scientific precision. I also thank those colleagues who encouraged me to embark on this project or helped bring it to completion: Robert Vosloo, Bill Everett, James Furr, Larry Rasmussen, Keith Clements, Ralf Wuestenberg, Zaineh Barakat, Christian McCabe, and Anton de Gruchy. And, as always, I am indebted to editor-in-chief K. C. Hanson and his colleagues at Cascade Books.

Going Against the Stream is a contribution to the celebration of the 80th anniversary of Dietrich Bonhoeffer's death on 9th April 1945. It is also offered in memory of Bonhoeffer's friend Eberhard and his niece Renate Bethge who befriended Isobel and me over many years. Also remembered is our son Steve who tragically died fifteen years ago but frequently reappears in these pages as a true dissenter. In remembering him Isobel and I give thanks to his siblings and his family who continue to bring us joy. Judy and Julian Cooke have been our companions on many journeys including that of faith. Julian died shortly before I finished writing this book having wonderfully embodied what Bonhoeffer called a genuinely "aesthetic existence."

John de Gruchy
Volmoed
August 2025

Abbreviations

AB	Anchor Bible
ABM	American Board of Commissioners for Foreign Missions
AI	Artificial Intelligence
AIC	African Indigenous Churches
AGI	Artificial General Intelligence
ANC	African National Congress
BCC	Bantu Congregational Church
CI	Christian Institute
CUSA	Congregational Union of South Africa
CCRAI	*Cambridge Companion to Religion and Artificial Intelligence*. Edited by Beth Singler and Fraser Watts. Cambridge Companions to Religion. Cambridge: Cambridge University Press, 2024
DBWE	Dietrich Bonhoeffer Works in English
DRC	Dutch Reformed Church
LMS	London Missionary Society
LCC	Library of Christian Classics
NIGTC	New International Greek Testament Commentary
SACC	South African Council of Churches
STJ	*Stellenbosch Theological Journal*

ABBREVIATIONS

TDNT   *Theological Dictionary of the New Testament.* Edited by Gerhard Kittel and Gerhard Friedrich. Translated by Geoffrey W. Bromiley. 10 vols. Grand Rapids: Eerdmans, 1964–1976

UCCSA   United Congregational Church of Southern Africa

WCC   World Council of Churches

Prologue
Living Between the Times

Have there ever been people in history who in their time, like us, had so little ground under their feet, people to whom every possible alternative open to them at the time appeared equally unbearable, senseless, and contrary to life?

—BONHOEFFER, "AFTER TEN YEARS"[1]

BONHOEFFER WROTE HIS ESSAY "After Ten Years" at the "turn of the year 1942–43" as a gift for his friends in the German Resistance. He begins with three questions. The first is whether there have ever been people in history who felt that there was "so little ground under their feet" that all the options left to them were "equally unbearable, senseless, and contrary to life." The second is whether they were "facing a great historical turning point" for which experience provides little guidance. The third and "ultimately responsible question" is how the "coming generation is to go on living" because only "from such a historically responsible question will fruitful solutions arise."[2] With these questions in mind allow me to inject my autobiography into the narrative as partner in the conversation that follows.

1. Bonhoeffer, *Letters and Papers*, 38.
2. Bonhoeffer, *Letters and Papers*, 42.

Going Against the Stream

I was born in 1939 shortly before the outbreak of the Second World War and now, as my life comes to its conclusion, many of us fear that we are on the brink of a third world war. Looking back to my mother's birth in 1900 during the Anglo-Boer War, it also seems as if war is normal and peace a brief and infrequent interlude. Yet there is a difference between war more than a century ago and now, for with each outbreak of war, new technologies are developed to crush the enemy, but this development massively diverts scarce resources from pursuing peace and saving an ailing planet. It was only yesterday that the world seemed to be becoming a better habitat for humanity; today it appears to be on the brink of mass destruction.

Those who read the Bible will know that this foreboding sense of living between the times is located within a cosmic narrative of creation and redemption. Within this immense landscape the human story is told in such a way that, despite much evidence to the contrary, it evokes trust in God as the mystery in which "we live, move and have our being." Within this framework, in which myth informs history and history makes myth real, God calls us to live and work in anticipation of a world of justice and peace. At the center of this narrative is the good news that God's mystery and redemptive love for the world have been disclosed in Jesus of Nazareth. This offers hope for the world without minimizing the oppressive suffering that accompanies the coming of God's reign.

So, we live between the times: between the cosmic origin of the world and its demise, between our birth and death, and also, as it happens in my case, between the beginning of a lifelong conversation with Bonhoeffer and its ending. And as I do, I listen with Bonhoeffer to what the Spirit is saying to us about how we should live in the world today for the sake of future generations.[3]

In response, Bonhoeffer—ever the hopeful realist—says that while it seems "more sensible to be pessimistic . . . no one ought to despise optimism as the will for the future, however many times it is mistaken." He then writes words that have been imprinted on my mind since I first read them during the church struggle

---

3. De Gruchy, *Bonhoeffer's Questions*, 18–21.

against apartheid.[4] "There are people," he writes, "who think it frivolous and Christians who think it impious to hope for a better future on earth and to prepare for it. They believe in chaos, disorder, and catastrophe, perceiving it in what is happening now." So, "they resign themselves to their fate or piously withdraw from any responsibility for the future." Of course, Bonhoeffer concludes, the "day of judgment" might "dawn tomorrow," but only when it does will he give up working for a "better future."[5] These words came to mind when, shortly after Donald Trump was elected president of the United States for the first time, I wrote *The End Is Not Yet: Standing Firm in Apocalyptic Times*.[6] They are once again on my mind today though perhaps far more so.

---

4. See de Gruchy, "Bonhoeffer in South Africa"; and de Gruchy, "Providence and the Shapers of History."

5. Bonhoeffer, *Letters and Papers*, 51.

6. De Gruchy, *End Is Not Yet*.

1

Dissent in Christendom

> While the world imagines progress, strength, and a grand future, the disciples know about the end, judgment, and the arrival of the kingdom of heaven, for which the world is not at all ready. That is why the disciples are rejected as strangers in the world, bothersome guests, disturbers of the peace.
>
> —Bonhoeffer[1]

> Jesus also knows those others, the representatives and preachers of the national religion, those powerful, respected people, who stand firmly on the earth inseparably rooted in the national way of life, the spirit of the times, the popular piety. But Jesus does not speak to them; he speaks only to his disciples when he says, blessed—for theirs is the kingdom of heaven.[2]
>
> —Bonhoeffer

---

1. Bonhoeffer, *Discipleship*, 104
2. Bonhoeffer, *Discipleship*, 103.

THE YEAR 2025 IS auspicious in the Christian calendar for several reasons other than being the eightieth anniversary of Bonhoeffer's contentious martyrdom.[3] During this year, the ecumenical church celebrates the seventeenth centenary of the Nicene Creed, the Mennonites celebrate the five-hundredth anniversary of the birth of Anabaptism in Zurich in 1525, and some of us celebrate the fortieth anniversary of the publication of the *Kairos Document* in 1985.[4] I rejoice in all those celebrations for they have all influenced my life as a Christian dissenter and a student of Bonhoeffer's legacy. But I suspect few will join me in commemorating the hundred-fiftieth anniversary of the passing of the Voluntary Act by the Cape Parliament in 1875. I remember it because my journey as a Congregationalist is connected to this somewhat obscure footnote in South African history.[5] Another reason I do so is because Philippe Denis, a Catholic historian, has said that too little scholarly attention has been given to Congregationalism in South Africa despite its "rich and in some ways unique ecclesial tradition."[6]

As Denis wrote his essay in memory of our son Steve, the Congregational tradition he had in mind was that represented by the United Congregational Church of Southern Africa (UCCSA), of which Steve, like me, was also a minister. However, if Congregationalism is primarily understood as an ecclesial *polity* in which local congregations are autonomous, then it would be better represented today by Baptists and some independent churches. This is because the polity of the UCCSA has evolved over the past century within the context of southern Africa.[7] So, in reflecting on dissent in Christendom I begin with this nonconforming tradition, which I believe is more ecumenical rather than unique.

---

3. On Bonhoeffer as martyr, see Bethge, *Bonhoeffer*, 155–56; Slane, *Bonhoeffer as Martyr*.

4. Kairos Theologians, *Kairos Document*.

5. See Davenport, "Consolidation of a New Society," 285–86.

6. Denis, "Historical Roots of Southern African Congregationalism," 305.

7. See Briggs, *Covenant Church*.

Going Against the Stream

THE CONGREGATIONAL WAY

My attempt to understand the Congregational tradition began when, as a graduate student, I wrote a thesis titled "The Congregational Way" (1960).[8] A few years later I wrote a second thesis, "The Local Church and Racial Identity in South Africa" (1964), to better understand my role as a Congregational pastor in a racist society.[9] In the latter I drew greatly on Bonhoeffer's doctoral dissertation, *Sanctorum Communio*, which laid the foundation for his theological development and much of my own.[10] In fact, that was when I first began to enter into conversation with Bonhoeffer and realized that his foundational questions—"who is Jesus Christ for us today?" and therefore "what is the church?"—are precisely the core questions of the Congregational tradition, just as they always should be for the ecumenical church.[11]

Congregationalism emerged during the Protestant Reformation in England as part of a long dissenting tradition within Christendom, which followed the conversion of the Roman Emperor Constantine early in the fourth century. This epochal event, which eventually led to Christianity becoming the official imperial religion under Emperor Theodosius, transformed a persecuted sect into a rapidly growing state institution.[12] But it also provoked a dissenting tradition whose origins are found in the pre-Constantinian church and early monasticism.[13]

The first Congregationalists, known as Independents, regarded themselves as part of this ancient dissenting tradition, alongside Baptists and Quakers, all of whom rejected the Act of Uniformity adopted by the British Parliament in 1603. This Act required all citizens except Jews to become members of the Church

---

8. De Gruchy, "Congregational Way."
9. De Gruchy, "Local Church and Racial Identity."
10. Bonhoeffer, *Sanctorum Communio*; Green, *Bonhoeffer*.
11. See de Gruchy, *Bonhoeffer's Questions*, 21–23, 125–28.
12. On the complex origins and character of Christendom and its development to the Great Schism between Eastern Orthodoxy and the Roman Catholic Churches in the eleventh century, see Runciman, *Eastern Schism*.
13. See de Gruchy, *This Monastic Moment*, 14–15, 114–16.

of England. Roman Catholics refused, as did many Protestants, who collectively became known as Nonconformists or Dissenters.[14] By the seventeenth century, most Independent congregations were Calvinist in theology, in common with Presbyterians and evangelicals in the Church of England. But they differed in ecclesial polity, rejecting both episcopacy and Presbyterianism in favor of congregational autonomy subject only to Christ and the guidance of the Holy Spirit.

The Evangelical Revival led by John Wesley, which launched the Methodist movement in the eighteenth century, not only changed the social fabric of Britain but breathed new life into the Nonconformist churches. By then probably the majority were Independents or, as they were becoming known, Congregationalists. The Revival also awakened a social conscience that later in the nineteenth century became known as the Nonconformist Conscience, which championed religious liberty, educational reform, social morality, and temperance. But it also awoke an enthusiasm for the evangelization of the world, which led to the formation of the London Missionary Society (LMS) in 1795. Even though the majority of those involved in founding the LMS were Congregationalists, its stated purpose was not to export a denomination to foreign lands but to take Christ to the nations.[15]

DISSENT AT THE CAPE

From the time that the Cape of Good Hope was colonized by the Dutch East India Company in 1652, the Dutch Reformed Church (DRC) was in its employ under the watchful eye of a political commissar. Whatever benefits accrued to the church and no matter how devout its ministers and members, the DRC was a functionary of a globally expanding trading company.[16] When the Cape became a British colony in the early nineteenth century, the Church

14. See Munson, *Nonconformists*. See Grant, *Free Churchmanship in England 1870–1940*.
15. See de Gruchy, "Remembering a Legacy," 1.
16. See Nieder-Heitmann, "Christendom at the Cape."

of England became responsible for the spiritual well-being of a new cohort of settlers, officials, and soldiers subject to a colonial government whose reason for being at the cape was to protect British imperial ambitions. In short, the planting of Protestant Christendom at the Cape was a colonial project.

This project became increasingly complex under British control, for it opened the door to large numbers of European missionaries, who in the late eighteenth century began to trek into the interior where they established mission stations.[17] At the same time the colony became home to Scottish Presbyterians and British Nonconformists. There was also a growing Roman Catholic presence at the Cape which the strongly Protestant authorities regarded with considerable reservation if not hostility. In an attempt to avoid denominationalism, Congregationalists established the short-lived Evangelical Voluntary Union[18] in 1859 as a home for all English-speaking Nonconformists.[19] But irrespective of denomination, all churches were under the watchful eye of the governor-general, though none had the same political or social status as the dominant DRC or the established Church of England.[20]

In 1854, however, Saul Solomon, a Congregationalist member of the Cape Parliament, introduced a private member's bill in which he proposed that all churches in the colony should be independent of the state. This separation was necessary if the church was to "render to Caesar the things that are Caesar's" and especially "to God the things that are God's."[21] Despite such biblical support, Solomon's bill was strongly opposed by the DRC and the Anglicans, who even discussed uniting to form an established

---

17. See du Plessis, *History of Christian Missions in South Africa*.

18. "Evangelical" then simply meant Protestant or, as still today in Germany, *Evangelische*.

19. When that failed the Congregational Union of South Africa (CUSA) was established in 1877. See Ferguson, *CUSA*, 4-75. The Congregational Union of England and Wales, which was established in 1832, joined with the Presbyterian Church in England in 1972 to become the United Reformed Church.

20. See de Gruchy, *Christianity and the Modernisation of South Africa*.

21. Mark 12:17 (KJV).

colonial church.²² But Solomon persisted until, in May 1875, the Voluntary Act was narrowly passed when the speaker cast his vote in favor. One reason for the support now given by Anglicans was the growing resistance among "high church" Tractarians to state interference in church affairs, which reached boiling point in the heresy trial of the bishop of Natal, John Colenso.²³ Even so, some Anglicans had done the unthinkable and sided with Dissent.²⁴ In doing so, they were not just supporting Solomon's bill, but tacitly acknowledging that Dissent was not heresy or schismatic, but an attempt to obey and follow Christ rather than submit to the cultural elite and politically powerful.

Saul Solomon was a member of Union Church in Cape Town, a congregation established in 1820 by Dr. John Philip to serve Congregational and Presbyterian settlers and soldiers. Philip, a Scot by birth, was the superintendent of the LMS, which was pioneering missionary work in the colony. As superintendent he was, by necessity if not by title, a Nonconformist "bishop." Missionary endeavor obviously required a strategic change in Congregational polity if it was to succeed. But whatever his title or role, according to Lord Charles Somerset, the governor-general, Philip was an "arrant dissenter" like all those who refused to be co-opted by the government.²⁵ Indeed, after the war between the British Colonial forces and the Ama-Xhosa on the Eastern Cape frontier (1834–1836), Philip testified before the British Parliament, blaming Britain for the conflict.

Unsurprisingly, then, Somerset's dislike of Dissenters was shared by most aristocratic Anglicans in England, for whom they were radicals and heretics bent on controlling the House of Commons and disestablishing the Church of England. But Philip was no radical or heretic; he was a dogged Scots Calvinist like his

---

22. De Gruchy, *Church Struggle in South Africa* (2nd ed., 1986), 17

23. See Hinchliff, *Anglican Church in South Africa*, 87–100.

24. On the Church of England and Dissent in England during this period, see Chadwick, *Victorian Church. Part 1*, 60–100.

25. See Keegan, *Dr Philip's Empire*, 81–95.

colleague John Read,[26] both of whom challenged Somerset's racial policies and worked for the emancipation of slaves in support of William Wilberforce, an Anglican evangelical in England. It had become impossible for Philip to "take Christ to the nations" and save the souls of the "heathen" without also working for their liberation. This is a reminder that evangelical Christianity as expressed by Wesley, Wilberforce, and Philip, and behind them by Count Zinzendorf, the founder of the Moravian movement in Germany, was in the forefront of the struggle for social justice long before much evangelical Christianity in modern-day America was highjacked in the interests of Christian nationalism.[27]

In 1839, following the British Act of Emancipation, Philip founded another congregation in Cape Town, this time for freed slaves in District Six where his wife, Jane, as doughty a Dissenter as John, established a school for their children.[28] Her legacy later inspired Emilie Jane Solomon, Saul's granddaughter and a deacon in the Sea Point Congregational Church, to become a leading activist in South Africa for women's rights, irrespective of race, in the 1930s. In 1937 Emilie was also elected chair of the Congregational Union of South Africa (CUSA), the first woman to lead a denomination in the country,[29] though the Anglican dean of Cape Town at that time said that the whole Christian church was indebted to her leadership.[30]

---

26. John Read was a Congregationalist, LMS missionary and antislavery activist. In 1800 he founded the Calvinist Society in Cape Town. See de Gruchy, "Dissenting Calvinism."

27. See Kaylor and Underwood, *Baptizing America*.

28. See Villa-Vicencio and Grassow, *Christianity and the Colonisation of South Africa*, 56–58; Erlank, "Jane and John Philip," 82–98.

29. See Carson, *Emilie Solomon*; Briggs and Wing, *Harvest and the Hope*, 292–93.

30. Carson, *Emilie Solomon*, 40.

A DISSENTER BY DEFAULT

The fact that I grew up in Union Congregational Church of which John Philip was the founding pastor and Saul Solomon a member was a matter of convenience for my Methodist parents, who, at the insistence of my maternal grandparents, named me John Wesley at my baptism. But Union Church was the nearest Nonconformist church to where we lived in Cape Town, it had a lively youth program, and (as my parents said) we all sang the same hymns.[31] Convenient it was, but their decision was providential, for it introduced me to the legacy of the Philips at a formative stage in my life.

I first learned the story of the Philips' missionary labors and struggles against slavery from reading their plaques on the sanctuary wall facing the pulpit at Union Church, but I doubt whether the story had much traction on the life of the congregation. Union Church was a typical English-speaking colonial congregation living in a middle-class racial bubble and nurtured on a liberal theology that made few demands beyond moral behavior. Despite that, no one could easily erase the witness of the Philip plaques, and one day I would appreciate the fact that John Philip was not only a Congregationalist and evangelical Dissenter but also a pioneer of a liberating Reformed tradition that became part of my inheritance.[32]

None of this would have happened, however, if I had not accepted the challenge to commit my life to Jesus Christ at a Scripture Union camp in 1953.[33] Soon after, I was encouraged by a school friend to be rebaptized in a Plymouth Brethren chapel.[34] The Brethren, whose origins in England were evangelical Anglican, also tried to convince me to leave Union Church, but I declined. Nonetheless by being rebaptized I had become an Anabaptist long before I knew the word, discovered its connection to Congregationalism, or learned about its radical challenge

---

31. See de Gruchy, *I Have Come a Long Way*, 29–30.
32. See de Gruchy, *Liberating Reformed Theology*, 42–44.
33. See de Gruchy, *I Have Come a Long Way*, 36–37.
34. On the Plymouth Brethren, see Durnbaugh, *Believers' Church*, 161–72.

to the churches of Christendom. The Brethren also introduced me to the dispensationalist eschatology of John Darby, who claimed that Jesus would shortly return to save those who believed. I had never heard anything like this from the pulpit of Union Church where I learned that the kingdom of God is within us and that our task was to spread God's reign across the world. In fact, I do not recall any sense of "living between the times" whether with reference to Darby, or in a very different way, to Barth, for whom it was fundamental for doing theology and Christian dissent in Nazi Germany.[35]

Darby's views, which resembled those of the medieval Franciscan friar Girolama Savonarola and other radical Catholic Dissenters in the sixteenth century, have had a significant influence on Christian fundamentalism in South Africa and elsewhere, and today contribute to the rise of Christian Zionism and Christian nationalism.[36] Intrigued as I was by Darby's teaching, I did not follow that path, but I now understand why dispensationalism has such an attraction for people living in uncertain and fearful times, and how it influences local and global politics.

My parents were perplexed by my youthful religious zeal, and my rebaptism caused them some consternation, though I later discovered that some great Reformed theologians also had reservations about infant baptism.[37] But to my surprise Basil Brown, the minister at Union Church, took no steps to discipline me for having been rebaptized; on the contrary he sensed that I had a call to the ministry. Discovering this, my parents asked me if I would not prefer to become a Methodist rather than a Congregational minister, to which I replied, "I prefer to stick with what I am despite my baptismal name!" The truth is, I did not know the difference; I had

---

35. See Gorringe, *Karl Barth: Against Hegemony*, 74–116.

36. See Jansen, "Influence of Fundamentalism on Evangelicalism in South Africa"; Marsden, *Fundamentalism and American Culture*; and McCrummen, "Army of God."

37. See Schleiermacher, *Christian Faith*, 637; Barth, *Church Dogmatics*, IV/I, *Doctrine of Reconciliation*, 78–194.

become a Dissenter by default and was on my way to becoming a Reformed one by conviction.

AFRIKANER REFORMED DISSENT

Brown studied at the University of Cape Town before going to Mansfield College, Oxford, which was, in the 1930s, a major Congregational theological college in England. It was there that he experienced the tension between those Congregationalists who were liberal Protestants influenced by Adolf von Harnack, one of Bonhoeffer's illustrious teachers in Berlin, and a post–First World War generation who were attracted to the theology of Karl Barth, Bonhoeffer's unofficial mentor.[38] For the former, the focus was on following the "Jesus of history"; for Barth, who had been nurtured on such liberal theology, this was totally inadequate for the crisis that faced Christendom on the outbreak of the First world War. Instead, he went back to the Bible and Calvin, and under the sway of Søren Kierkegaard's *Attack on Christendom*, sought to discern how the church should respond and ended up going against the stream.[39]

Brown considered Barth's Calvinism to be much the same as that which supported Afrikaner nationalism. But this was both a failure on his part to understand Barth and recognize the diversity within the Reformed tradition that traces its heritage back to the Swiss Reformation. Congregationalists are certainly Calvinists by tradition, but today far more moderately so than sometimes in the past. When true to the Reformed tradition, they have had a profound sense of both personal and social sin, of God's reign over human affairs, and of their calling to be responsible agents of God's will in society.[40] While this worldview is by no means distinct to

---

38. See Grant, *Free Churchmanship in England*, 374–76; Harnack, *What Is Christianity?*; Rumscheidt, *Revelation and Theology*.

39. Busch, *Karl Barth*, 81–108, 115; Kierkegaard, *Kierkegaard's Attack upon "Christendom."*

40. See McNeil, *History and Character of Calvinism*; de Gruchy *Liberating Reformed Theology*, 4–8; de Gruchy, *John Calvin*, 28–34, 219–28.

Calvinism, Calvin, like Saint Augustine, located it within a majestic interpretation of the core themes of Christian faith, earning him a place among the doctors of the ecumenical church.[41]

Afrikaner Calvinism had its roots in Dutch Calvinism, but in the late nineteenth and early twentieth centuries some DR theologians began to insist that the emerging Afrikaner volk was especially chosen by God to preserve Protestant Christendom in southern Africa.[42] This was, however, a folk-ideology with a "thin veneer of Calvinistic terminology and theological content" fashioned on the hostile frontiers of Dutch expansion in southern Africa.[43] As such, it was much like those theological ideologies that were used to justify the colonial expansion by other European powers, whether by the Catholic Spanish Conquistadors in Latin America in the sixteen century or English Puritans in New England in the seventeenth. Likewise, the victory in 1948 of the Afrikaner Nationalist Party, though clinched by the promise of white supremacy and security, would not have happened without the advocacy of the Dutch Reformed Church in South Africa. Similarly, today, Christian nationalism in the United States is informed by a combination of popular evangelical fundamentalism and an American exceptionalism based on a sense of divine calling to govern the world. It is precisely this Christendom conviction, which Bonhoeffer regarded as nothing but a triumphalist heresy, that has provided theological support for crusades, inquisitions, and pogroms in the name of Christ.[44]

Basil Brown seldom mentioned politics in his sermons. But I was proud to see him on the city hall platform during an anti-apartheid protest meeting I attended as a student at the University of Cape Town. I also remember discussing with him B. B. Keet's *Whither, South Africa?*, the first critique of apartheid from within the DRC.[45] Keet was then a senior professor in theology at

---

41. See Ganoczy, *Young Calvin*; see also de Gruchy, *John Calvin*, 113–32.
42. See Moodie, *Rise of Afrikanerdom*; de Klerk, *Puritans in Africa*.
43. Templin, *Ideology on a Frontier*, 313.
44. See Bosch, "Nothing but a Heresy."
45. Keet, *Whither, South Africa?*.

Stellenbosch University where, in 1959, I heard him lecture on Reformed theology over the previous century and recall the positive things he said about Barth's contribution. And it was under Barth's influence that Keet became critical of Afrikaner nationalism.[46]

A few months later, in May 1960, as I was finishing my thesis on "The Congregational Way," South Africa was shaken to the core by the Sharpeville massacre. In response, the World Council of Churches (WCC) hastily convened a consultation at Cottesloe in Johannesburg that December for all its South African member churches. The participants included delegates from the two largest synods of the DRC, one of which was led by Beyers Naudé, the moderator of the Northern Transvaal synod and a protégé of Keet, who played a crucial role at Cottesloe.[47]

Soon after Cottesloe, Basil Brown was elected president of the Christian Council of South Africa (1961–1962), and then its general secretary prior to it becoming the South African Council of Churches (SACC) in 1957. In that capacity he worked closely with the Anglican archbishop of Cape Town, Joost de Blank, an archenemy of the apartheid government, and drafted several council documents critical of apartheid legislation. Meanwhile, after Cottesloe, Naudé launched the ecumenical Christian Institute (CI) for which he was defrocked by the DRC.[48] He had become an Afrikaner dissenter, and a mentor for many of us.[49] Naudé was, as Bonhoeffer's friend Eberhard Bethge would later tell me during his visit to South Africa in 1973, "South Africa's Bonhoeffer."[50] And it was Naudé who encouraged me to write my doctoral dissertation on Bonhoeffer.[51] And that, of course, was when my conversation with Bonhoeffer, that had begun when I wrote my masters' thesis

---

46. De Gruchy, "Reception and Relevance of Karl Barth in South Africa."

47. Hewson, ed., *Cottesloe Consultation*.

48. See de Gruchy, "Short History of the Christian Institute."

49. See Durand, "Afrikaner Piety and Dissent,"; Saayman, "Rebels and Prophets"; Boesak *Black and Reformed*.

50. See de Gruchy, "Beyers Naudé"; de Gruchy, *Daring, Trusting Spirit*, 161.

51. De Gruchy, "Dynamic Structure of the Church."

in Chicago, began to gather a momentum that has never slowed down.

In 1968 I accepted an invitation from Bishop Bill Burnett, another participant at Cottesloe, and the first general secretary of the SACC, to join its staff in Braamfontein, Johannesburg, which was located close to Naudé's Christian Institute (CI). I commenced work there that April during the week in which the CI and SACC jointly published the "Message to the People of South Africa," which declared that apartheid was a "false gospel."[52] This was a prophetic milestone in the church struggle, but largely the work of white, anti-apartheid theologians. As such it was soon overshadowed by the emergence of the Black Consciousness Movement led by Steve Biko and the Black Theology Project, whose office was located just above mine during 1972.

For Black theology, Christ was unashamedly Black, with all that implied both for those under the yoke of apartheid and for the white-controlled churches. To the significance of this development, especially after the Soweto Uprising in 1976, I shall return. For me, it was already clear that white-dominated, ecumenical anti-apartheid initiatives were unlikely to succeed in an apartheid society. I was also beginning to acknowledge that the European and North American theology on which I was nurtured had to be critically reimagined in response to Black theology if it was to become relevant. But that was not yet on my mind when in 1965 I gave a lecture at the Federal Theological Seminary at Alice in the Eastern Cape where Black students trained for the ministry of the so-called English-speaking churches, and where Black theology would later take root.[53] Instead, my lecture was on the social witness of the church in the theology of P. T. Forsyth, a Scottish Congregationalist theologian of a previous generation, sometimes referred to as a "Barth before Barth."[54]

---

52. De Gruchy and de Villiers, eds., *Message in Perspective*.

53. See de Gruchy, *I Have Come a Long Way*, 68.

54. See Bradley, *P.T. Forsyth*; Rodgers, *Theology of P.T. Forsyth*; Sykes, "P.T. Forsyth."

Like Barth, Forsyth was schooled in nineteenth-century German liberal Protestant theology and Idealist philosophy. And like Barth a generation later, he found liberal theology inadequate to address the challenges presented by the First World War. And so, also under the influence of Kierkgaard, Forsyth turned to the message of the Bible and the Reformers for guidance.[55] Critical of both liberal theology and fundamentalism, Forsyth's Christocentric theology was, again like Barth's and Bonhoeffer's, ecclesially and socially engaged.[56] Forsyth's theology helped me better appreciate what Congregational Dissent was essentially about. It was Reformed in theology, but "Calvinism flushed and fertilized by Anabaptism on English ground."[57] Being Reformed meant that Congregationalists, unlike Anabaptists, were willing to participate in government and were not pacifists (Oliver Cromwell was a Congregationalist), but like Anabaptists, they refused political and therefore also episcopal interference in the life of the church. Their dissent was Reformed but not Radical. But could it be both?

RADICAL DISSENT

Although the Protestant Reformation was driven by theological convictions, its success depended on the support of like-minded princes and magistrates. This relationship was established at the Diet of Speyer in 1529 when several German princes pledged their allegiance to Martin Luther and Philip Melancthon in Wittenburg, and Swiss magistrates gave theirs to Ulrich Zwingli and Heinrich Bullinger in Zurich. In return, the Reformers acknowledged their authority in maintaining *Evangelische* Christendom. In contrast to these so-called Magisterial Reformers, a more radical and diverse group of leaders and their followers were inappropriately lumped

---

55. See *inter alia* Forsyth, *Justification of God*.

56. See Forsyth, *Person and Place of Jesus Christ*; Forsyth, *Socialism, the Church and the Poor*.

57. Forsyth, *Faith, Freedom and the Future*, 30.

together at Speyer, named Anabaptists, and collectively considered a threat to both the Reformation and Christendom.[58]

There was some substance to this fear. Four years previously, in 1525, a former Catholic priest named Thomas Müntzer, disillusioned with the slow speed and scope of Luther's reforms, had led the notoriously violent Peasants' Revolt in Mühlhausen, in Thuringia.[59] That same year, in Zurich, several followers of Zwingli, also a former priest, decided that his reforms were likewise too slow and not radical enough.[60] But, instead of trying to overthrow Christendom by force, they espoused pacifism and attempted to undermine it by rejecting infant baptism, which had become a sign of social conformity rather than one of faith and discipleship.

After lengthy disputations, the leaders of the Zurich dissidents in a dramatic act of defiance against Christendom and God-ordained authority, rebaptized themselves in a nearby river. This made Anabaptists heretics and subversives, who, like many others (from the Montanists in the second century to Savonarola in the Middle Ages), deserved the death penalty. But for Anabaptists, martyrdom (often by drowning) became a badge of honor because they believed they were being persecuted for confessing Jesus as Lord and seeking to live according to his teaching in a nominally Christian world.[61]

Most Anabaptist refugees went to Holland, which was a more tolerant Calvinist society than Switzerland, but they were in disarray and divided by theological disagreements. Fortuitously, another former Catholic priest, Menno Simons (1496–1561), had joined their ranks, become their leader, and built a more resilient "voluntary brotherhood of love and non-resistance" based on the Sermon of the Mount.[62] These Anabaptists, who were now becoming known as Mennonites, met some English Independents, who

---

58. See the Introduction to Williams, *Radical Reformation*, xxiii–xxxi.
59. See Gritsch, *Thomas Müntzer*.
60. Williams, *Radical Reformation*, 118–48; de Gruchy, *John Calvin*, 72–77.
61. See Blanke, "Anabaptism and the Reformation," 57–65.
62. See Krahn, *Dutch Anabaptism*; Bender, "Anabaptist Vision"; and van der Zijpp, "Early Dutch Anabaptists," 76–82.

had also fled persecution and settled in Holland.[63] Later, after returning to England, it was from their ranks that the Pilgrim Fathers sailed to America in 1620 and settled in New England where, ironically, they established a largely Congregational Puritan outpost of Christendom.[64]

Isobel and I experienced a residue of that status when I served as a summer supply pastor in 1964 at the Stockbridge Congregational Church in Massachusetts. On arrival we discovered that the second pastor of the church had been Jonathan Edwards (1703–1758), the famous Calvinist theologian and later the president of Princeton University. But before entering academia, Edwards led the First Great Awakening in America much as Wesley had led the Evangelical Revival in Britain. Central to Edwards's vision was a born-again America that would replace European Christendom after its predicted secular demise.[65] In this regard it is worth pondering what Bonhoeffer wrote in 1939 about Protestantism in the United States. "American Christianity," he said, "remains concealed from those who do not know the beginning of the Congregationalists in New England, the Baptists in Rhode Island, or the revival movement led by Jonathan Edwards."[66]

EXTENDING THE REIGN OF GOD

Just as the Evangelical Revival in England led to the formation of the LMS, so the Great Awakening inspired a missionary zeal that led to the formation of the American Board of Commissioners for Foreign Missions (ABM) in Boston in 1810. Twenty-two years later John Philip invited the ABM to send missionaries to southern Africa and in 1835 he welcomed them at the Cape before they headed north to establish mission stations in Zululand and

---

63. See Davies, *English Free Churches*, 20–62.
64. See Bainton, *Christian Unity and Religion in New England*; Handy, *Christian America*, viii–ix, 12–13.
65. See Miller, *Jonathan Edwards*; Jenson, *America's Theologian*.
66. Bonhoeffer, *Theological Education Underground*, 439.

elsewhere.[67] True to Edwards's vision they were convinced that their missionary labors would hasten the coming of God's kingdom and help complement the political mission of a young and burgeoning United States.[68]

A century and a half later the missions established by the ABM had become congregations and collectively part of the Bantu Congregational Church (BCC). Then, in 1967, the BCC united with the CUSA and the LMS churches in Botswana and Zimbabwe to form the UCCSA. In an act of inspiration, the UCCSA appointed Joseph Wing as its first general secretary, a position he held for twenty years. Wing was trained as a Congregational minister in England shortly after the Second World War. He was a Reformed pastor in the mold of P. T. Forsyth—a pacifist and conscientious objector in the Anabaptist tradition, and a LMS missionary like John Philip, who came to southern Africa in 1951 to work among the migrant mine laborers on the Witwatersrand.[69] He is remembered in South Africa for his remarkable contribution to the ecumenical movement, the church struggle against apartheid, and theological education.[70]

Wing's influence on the early formation and development of the UCCSA was immense, but I recall how he often said, Congregationalism is a polity designed for saints and there are few around. On a grander political stage, democracy is always in danger of being hijacked by populist tyranny, for its strength is also a potential Achilles' heel.[71] The truth is, whether in church or secular government, there is no perfect polity given human nature, even when the saints are committed to seek "the mind of Christ."[72]

Wing also knew that the future of the UCCSA lay in becoming a genuinely African church, not least because many African

67. See Christofersen, *Adventuring with God.*
68. Etherington, "Kingdoms of this World and the Next," 91.
69. See de Gruchy, "Remarkable Life."
70. See Archbishop Njongonkulu Ndungane's Foreword in *Spirit Undaunted.*
71. See de Gruchy, *Christianity and Democracy,* 6–21.
72. 1 Cor 2:16.

converts to Christianity had become disillusioned with the white control of the missionary societies, including the ABM and LMS. In fact, this had led some to establish their own independent churches,[73] which then developed into the enormous African Indigenous Church (AIC) movement in southern Africa.[74]

Labeled "separatist" by the South African government, like the radical Dissenters in seventeenth-century England had been, the AICs were considered a threat to political stability in the twentieth century. But their chief aim was to restore primitive Christianity free from European patronage, and many of them signaled this break with Christendom through rebaptism. Given this affinity with Anabaptism, it is not surprising that years later, American Mennonite missionaries in southern Africa entered a partnership with some AICs. I discovered this to my surprise when early in 1973 I was the guest speaker at a conference in Swaziland of Mennonite mission workers from across the region.[75]

That brief encounter led to an invitation to spend a month teaching a course on Bonhoeffer at Bethel College, a Mennonite institution in North Newton, Kansas, in January 1975, and a further invitation to give the Menno Simons Lectures there in 1977.[76] These lectures on the church struggle against apartheid evoked considerable interest not least because they were given shortly after the globally reported Soweto Uprising, the state murder of the Black Consciousness leader Steve Biko, and the banning of Beyers Naudé.[77] Two years later the lectures reached a wider audience when they were published as *The Church Struggle in South Africa* in the US, South Africa, and Britain.[78]

---

73. See de Gruchy, ed., *Changing Frontiers*.

74. See Sundkler, *Bantu Prophets in South Africa*, 44–46; de Gruchy, *Church Struggle in South Africa* (2nd ed.), 41–50; and de Gruchy, *Christianity and the Modernisation of South Africa*, 12–18.

75. See Oduro et al., eds., *Unless a Grain of Wheat*.

76. De Gruchy, *I Have Come a Long Way*, 86–87, 101–11.

77. See Karis et al., eds., *From Protest to Challenge*, 5:551–95, 741–48.

78. De Gruchy, *Church Struggle in South Africa* (1st ed., 1979).

This, my first major book, was generally well received, but it also attracted some criticism to which I responded in a postscript to the second edition. And, then, twenty-five years later, our son Steve, who as a high school student had heard the lectures at Bethel College and since then had become an accomplished historian and theologian, suggested that we jointly publish a third, anniversary edition in which criticisms could be more fully addressed.[79] We also replaced the final chapter on "The Kingdom of God in South Africa" with two new chapters. In the first I discussed the church struggle during the final years of resistance and the transition to democracy; in the second, Steve related the struggle in South Africa to the global struggles facing the church in the post-apartheid era.[80] In addition, in a historiographical evaluation of the original book he concluded that it was neither theology or history as generally understood, but, "a contribution to the struggle and an invitation to others to participate in it." It was as much a sermon as it was history and theology.[81] He was, I think, correct in his assessment.

The only criticism I received of this third edition came in a doctoral dissertation on my theology in which, referring to the exclusion of the original concluding chapter, I was accused of reneging on my commitment to pacifism by giving tacit support to the armed liberation struggle in South Africa.[82] As a matter of fact, the chapter referred to was excluded for reasons of space not substance, but I regret that we excised it, for it relates to the current resurgence of Christian nationalism and the need for active resistance to war.

---

79. See de Gruchy and de Gruchy, *Church Struggle in South Africa* (3rd, 25th ann. ed., 2004), xxi–xxvi. Steve, who also became a Congregational minister and theologian, and was influenced by the Mennonites. See Cochrane et al., eds., *Living on the Edge*.

80. See de Gruchy and de Gruchy, *Church Struggle in South Africa* (3rd, 25th ann. ed., 2004), chs. 5 and 6.

81. Steve de Gruchy, "Locating *The Church Struggle in South Africa*." While there were many references to Bonhoeffer in the first edition, chiefly in the final chapter, there were very few in this third edition.

82. See Porteus, "Seeking the Dawn."

When the first edition was written, conscientious objection to military service was one of the few ways in which young white male South Africans could resist the apartheid state. Steve was one of a handful who did, mindful that refusal to serve in the army was one of the ways Christians from the outset have expressed dissent in Christendom. Some were also influenced by Bonhoeffer's understanding of "true patriotism."[83] This can be dated back to Bonhoeffer's year of study at Union Seminary in New York in 1930–1931 when, under the influence of a French fellow student and friend, Jean Lassere, he became a committed pacifist.[84] But clearly when he later joined the Resistance, he was no longer a pacifist in an absolute sense even though he remained committed to peacemaking, which is why he wanted to go to India and learn from Gandhi about active nonviolent resistance.[85] Understandably, my Mennonite friends found it difficult to reconcile Bonhoeffer's involvement in the plot to assassinate Hitler with his exposition of Jesus's Sermon on the Mount in *Discipleship*.[86] This led to robust conversations between us and made me rethink my own position.[87]

In 1984 I discussed this with Franz Hildebrandt, one of Bonhoeffer's closest friends during the German *Kirchenkampf* (Church Struggle). Hildebrandt spent several weeks with Bonhoeffer in London in 1933 when he was writing *Discipleship*, "the one book" said Hildebrandt, which Bonhoeffer "treasured above all others."[88] Shortly after that visit, Bonhoeffer told a friend in Germany that "the real struggle" facing the church was not just confessing its faith, but in "suffering through faith." "*Following* Christ" he wrote,

83. Clements, *Patriotism for Today*.

84. See Bethge, *Dietrich Bonhoeffer*, 153–54; Bonhoeffer, *Discipleship*, 290–91.

85. See Bonhoeffer, *London*, 81, 137; Prüller-Jagenteufel, "Dietrich Bonhoeffer."

86. See Bender, "Anabaptist Vision."

87. See de Gruchy, "Radical Peace-Making." Ironically, while there were many references to Bonhoeffer in the first edition of *The Church Struggle*, chiefly in the disputed final chapter, there were very few in this third edition.

88. Hildebrandt, "Oasis of Freedom," 39.

"is not exhausted" by the doctrine of justification by faith alone.[89] All of this was confirmed when I later read Hildebrandt's dissertation "Gospel and Humanitarianism" (1942), in which he argued that the failure of the Lutheran Church to exercise a prophetic witness in Nazi Germany was a consequence of its rejection of the witness of the Anabaptists.[90]

Bonhoeffer's later reservations about *Discipleship* as expressed in his prison letters was not a retraction of costly discipleship, as assumed by some, but a concern that his book might be misread in support of an otherworldly pietism. He considered the attempt to assassinate Hitler a necessary act of free responsibility despite the guilt it would incur.[91] And that was the reason why many Christians eventually supported the armed struggle against apartheid. But to understand this better we need to take a few steps back into history.

POLITY AND PROPHECY

From its formation in 1912, the African National Congress (ANC) had been committed to nonviolent resistance in the tradition of Ghandi, and Albert Luthuli, a former ANC president and a Congregationalist from Natal, was among its most vocal advocates.[92] So, when the leadership of the ANC decided to embark on the armed struggle in 1961, it did so only when it seemed that all other options over the past half century had failed.[93] It was not that pacifist resistance had failed after a few years, but after many

---

89. Bonhoeffer, *London*, 135.

90. See de Gruchy, *I Have Come a Long Way*, 136. Hildebrandt, "Gospel and Humanitarianism." I was asked to write an introduction when it was, unsuccessfully, submitted for publication in 1985. This was later published as de Gruchy, "Anticipating Liberation Theology."

91. See de Gruchy, *Bonhoeffer's Questions*, 141–43; see also de Gruchy, "Dietrich Bonhoeffer, Nelson Mandela"; and Clements, *Patriotism for Today*.

92. Luthuli, *Let My People Go*.

93. See Matthews, "Road from Nonviolence to Violence": see also my comparative discussion of Nelson Mandela and Bonhoeffer in de Gruchy, *Bonhoeffer's Questions*, 155–59.

years, which included futile visits to London to discuss the issues with its leaders, only to be rebuffed and ignored.

As many ANC members were also Christians, this decision inevitably implicated the churches before it erupted in public.[94] But it did do so with a vengeance following the decision of the World Council of Churches (WCC) in 1970 to launch its Program to Combat Racism (PCR) and provide humanitarian support to the liberation movements in southern Africa.[95]

As far as the apartheid government and most white members of the WCC's member churches in South Africa, including the UCCSA, were concerned, this decision implied support for the violent overthrow of the government. Pressure from Black members ensured that all the WCC member churches resisted the government's attempt to get them to resign their membership, though they did disassociate from the implied support for revolutionary violence. Despite this qualification, several congregations withdrew in protest from the UCCSA in 1977, one of them being Union Church, whose leadership barred Joseph Wing and me from addressing a meeting of the congregation. We were now persona non grata in the congregation in which I had first imbibed the dissenting legacy of John and Jane Philip. Congregational polity, reinforced by racism, made schism possible.

When the UCCSA was formed in 1967, congregations of the former Congregational Union (CUSA) retained their autonomy regarding finance and property, whereas those which were previously LMS and ABM mission congregations never had such autonomy. This meant that the former, which included all historically white settler congregations, had the power to withhold financial support from the UCCSA if they disagreed with its policies, and even to withdraw entirely and take their property with them. In effect, the UCCSA could be held for ransom by the white minority. This possibility was later changed by constitutional amendments, which in effect changed historic congregational polity on such matters. The fact is, Congregationalism was a polity originally

---

94. See de Gruchy, *I Have Come a Long Way*, 67–68.
95. De Gruchy, *Church Struggle in South Africa* (2nd ed.), 127–47.

adopted to prevent state interference not prophetic witness. The way dissent is embodied, as Bonhoeffer would have said, is contextual not absolute, which was his concern about "the relapse" of the Confessing Church into "conservative restoration" and forgetting about "genuine prophecy."[96] The white membership of the UCCSA had yet to be liberated from a colonial mentality and to become part of an African-led church.[97]

Shortly after the Soweto Uprising a youth contingent from UCCSA congregations in Soweto addressed our annual Assembly meeting in Durban. After sharing some of their harrowing experiences they posed a challenging question: if the church had declared apartheid unjust, and previously supported the "just war" against Hitler, how could it not support those who chose to fight now against apartheid by joining the liberation struggle? Certainly, the churches, whether Anglican or Nonconformist, were not pacifists, and they had invariably supported Britain not only in European wars, but also in the South African war against the Afrikaner Republics.[98] Thus, the challenge of the Soweto youth was not one that could be brushed aside; we had to face it as a denomination and in local congregations.

One of those congregations that accepted the challenge was the Rondebosch Congregational Church, which we had joined when I began teaching at the University of Cape Town in mid-1973. Like Union Church, Rondebosch had a liberal theological ethos but located near the university, it attracted more progressive students and faculty. In 1979, as the debate over the Program to Combat Racism was intensifying, the congregation called a Presbyterian, Douglas Bax, to become its minister. After graduating from Rhodes University, Bax had studied further at Princeton Theological Seminary and under Barth in Basel. He had also published a devastating biblical and theological critique of apartheid and had no hesitation in addressing political issues

---

96. See Bonhoeffer, *Letters and Papers*, 429

97. See de Gruchy, "Conversion & the Persistence of Colonial Racism."

98. See de Gruchy, *Christianity and the Modernisation of South Africa*, 52–60, 103–6.

from the pulpit.⁹⁹ This, together with his biblical exegetical style of preaching, was strong meat for many in the congregation, and several migrated elsewhere. At the same time, it attracted students, including some Baptists, who, like our son Steve, were facing military service, and for whom conscientious objection had become an act of resistance. In 1988, to protest the failure of the UCCSA and Presbyterian Church of Southern Africa to unite after years of negotiations, the congregation surrendered some of its autonomy when it voted to become the Rondebosch United Church (Congregational/Presbyterian), just as the church struggle against apartheid took a decisive new turn.

Back in 1982, the Black Dutch Reformed Mission Church had adopted the Belhar Confession, modeled on the Barmen Declaration drafted by Barth at the start of the German Church Struggle in 1934. Belhar declared that the theological legitimation of apartheid was a heresy, a decision that was endorsed by the UCCSA.¹⁰⁰ This meant that the DRC, which a century previously had adopted segregation as church polity and established racially stratified mission churches, was now being challenged from within its own family. This became even more problematic for the white DRC when some ministers within the Dutch Reformed Mission Church led by Allan Boesak, an outspoken prophet against apartheid, became actively involved in the United Democratic Front, which was engaged in large-scale acts of nonviolent resistance at the same time that the external liberation struggle was intensifying. In response, the government declared a draconian state of emergency in 1985 that lasted for several years.

This was the context within which an ecumenical group of theologians led by Albert Nolan, a Catholic Dominican theologian and Frank Chikane, a Pentecostal minister, met in Soweto to draft the *Kairos Document*, whose fortieth anniversary has also been celebrated in 2025. Arguing that theology had become a site of the struggle against apartheid, the *Kairos Document* rejected "state

---

99. Bax, *Different Gospel*.

100. See de Gruchy and Villa-Vicencio, eds., *Apartheid Is a Heresy*, 168; Cloete and Smit, eds., *Moment of Truth*.

theology," which gave Christian legitimacy to apartheid. It also rejected "church theology," which proclaimed "cheap reconciliation" without working for justice and liberation. Instead, it offered a "prophetic theology," which called the church to stand in solidarity with the liberation struggle. This was more radical than any previous theological attack on apartheid and immediately caused a political and ecclesiastical furor.[101]

Some of us who endorsed the *Kairos Document* did, however, express reservations about its use of the term "church theology." After all, the Belhar Confession demonstrated that church theology could be prophetic by rejecting apartheid as church policy.[102] This disagreement among supporters of the *Kairos Document* highlighted an important difference between understanding the church as an institution or, in a more Reformed way, as existing only truly where and when "the Word is faithfully proclaimed."[103] This helps us understand why, after the transition to democracy in 1994, the ecumenical church (understood as an institution) was regarded as having failed to speak truth to the new ANC government.[104]

Speaking truth to power only when necessary requires embodying the truth at all times.[105] As Bonhoeffer wrote during the German Church Struggle, the real struggle facing the church is not just confessing its faith when faced with a crisis, but in following Christ all the time.[106] To declare apartheid a "heresy" was

---

101. See de Gruchy and de Gruchy, *Church Struggle in South Africa* (3rd, 25th ann. ed., 2004), 184–222; de Gruchy, "Bonhoeffer's Legacy and Kairos-Palestine"; de Gruchy, "Kairos Moments and Prophetic Witness."

102. See de Gruchy, "On Being a Prophetic Church at *This Kairos* Moment"; Conradie, "Liberation, Reconciliation or Transformation?" Reservations about "church theology" were avoided in the *Kairos-Palestine Document* (2009) endorsed by the Orthodox Patriarchs and Heads of Churches in Palestine. See Balcomb and Denis, "Introduction."

103. See de Gruchy, "From *Kairos* to Belhar."

104. See Suderman, "Character and Potential Pitfalls of Prophetic Theology." This was an important Anabaptist contribution to the debate.

105. See de Gruchy, *Reconciliation*, 79–112.

106. Bonhoeffer, *Ethics*, 96–97.

necessary, but if the polity of the church is shaped by injustice, then the existence of the church becomes heretical. This was the struggle in the early church between the Judaizers and those who wanted to include Gentiles, and it remains the struggle whenever culture or ethnicity determines the structure of the church. Orthodoxy or "right belief" and orthopraxis or "right action" are inseparable, which is why Bonhoeffer's inseparable questions "who is Christ for us today?" and therefore "what is the church?" are as pertinent for today as they were when the bishops of the ecumenical church assembled at the ecumenical Council of Nicaea in 325.

ORTHODOX DISSENT

The birth of Christendom in the fourth century led many Christians to believe that God's reign had been established on earth.[107] They no longer had to fear the state or live in apocalyptic expectation. Bishop Eusebius of Caesarea even agreed with the emperor when he insisted that he was also a bishop ordained by God to establish a Christian empire and govern the whole world (*ecumene*) on God's behalf.[108] This implied that there was no contradiction in confessing Jesus as Lord and acknowledging the emperor as God's regent on earth at the same time.

However, Constantine knew that if Christianity was to replace the pagan deities of the past and become the spiritual glue that held the empire together, it was essential that the church should be united in faith. To this end, Constantine convened the Council at Nicaea in 325 to resolve the Arian controversy, which was tearing both the church and the empire apart. Named after Arius, an ascetic and learned priest in Alexandria, Arianism insisted that while Jesus is the Son of God, he is subordinate to God the Father.[109] Many Christians accepted Arianism as reasonable, and it appeared to be supported from some New Testament texts.

---

107. See Grant, *Augustus to Constantine*.

108. See Stevenson, ed., *New Eusebius*, 390–95.

109. See Frend, *Rise of Christianity*, 473–517; see Grillmeier, *Christ in Christian Tradition*, vol. 1, *From the Apostolic Age to Chalcedon*.

Nevertheless, it was challenged by Arius's bishop, Alexander, and by his young advisor and eventual successor, Athanasius.

Athanasius played a major role at the Council of Nicaea and was responsible for drafting the Nicene Creed, which several decades later shortly after Athanasius's death, was confirmed at the Council of Constantinople in 381. Officially known as the Nicene-Constantinopolitan Creed, it became the doctrinal basis of Christian orthodoxy. But from the outset there was much disagreement on how to interpret the relationship between the two natures of Christ, and between Jesus's suffering and death and his status as "truly God".[110] While such issues were clarified at the Council of Chalcedon in 451, the clarification did not satisfy all—hence the early schism between Eastern (Greek) and Oriental (Armenian, Syrian, Coptic, and Ethiopian) Orthodoxy.

However, Emperor Theodosius declared that only crazy people and heretics would not accept the Nicene Creed and ominously added that they deserved to be punished by the state on the authority of God if they rejected it.[111] After all, if Saint Peter was the rock on which the church was built, the emperor was the rock on which the empire was founded—a claim that turned out to be "a volcano whose eruptions could convulse the Church at any time."[112] For, once secular authority is accepted as a "divine right," then emperors and monarchs begin to rule in a way that is no different from deified pagan rulers. Such idolatry is why Christian nationalism has become a triumphalist heresy, and why Eastern Orthodoxy has become compromised by nationalism in eastern Europe since the collapse of the Soviet Union.[113]

This is also why Bonhoeffer's theology remains as pertinent today as it was in 1933 when he gave his lectures on Christology

---

110. See Bonhoeffer's discussion on Chalcedon in his "Lectures on Christology," 350–53.

111. Cochrane, *Christianity and Classical Culture*, 327.

112. Grillmeier, *Christ in Christian Tradition*, vol. 2, pt. 1, *From Chalcedon to Justinian*, 209.

113. Clements, "Dialogue with the Orthodox World, 342, 351–52; Clements, "'Dialogue or Confession?'"

in Berlin.[114] In them he dealt at length with the development of Christology up to the Council of Chalcedon before turning to consider Christology's contemporary significance. All of this must be assumed when later, in prison, he described Jesus as "the human being for others" and said that the church can therefore only be the church of Christ if it "exists for others" and confronts "the worship of power" by bearing witness to "the humanity of Jesus."[115] This was by no means a denial of the divinity of Christ; it was a recognition that God's power is revealed in the "weakness" of the cross,[116] echoing Martin Luther's *theologia crucis* against the *theologia gloriae* of Caeseropapism.[117] The only Christ who should determine the form and mission of the church is the One who was crucified, for this is the *only* Christ who is risen and glorified.[118]

After a detailed examination of the complexities of the Arian controversy, Rowan Williams, with due caution, has compared it to the German Church Struggle against National Socialism in the 1930s.[119] In both cases the major issue at stake was the uniqueness of God's self-revelation in Jesus Christ. Whatever their differences within the triune God, the *personae* are not separate individuals but consubstantial and united in creation and redemption. This means that no "order of creation," such as nation or ethnicity, is entitled to our unconditional loyalty, only the God revealed in Jesus Christ. As the Barmen Declaration, largely Barth's handiwork, put it, because "Jesus Christ . . . is the one Word of God," we must reject "other happenings and powers, images and truths, as divine revelation."[120] Or, as the Belhar Confession later said, the

114. Bonhoeffer, *Barcelona, Berlin, New York*, 299–360; See also de Gruchy, *Bonhoeffer's Questions*, 48–52.

115. Bonhoeffer, *Letters and Papers*, 503–4.

116. 1 Cor 1:18–25

117. See Luther, "Heidelberg Disputation, 1518" in Lull, ed., *Martin Luther's Basic Theological Writings*, 30–49; Loewenich, *Luther's Theology of the Cross*.

118. Phil 2:5–11; See also Moltmann, *Crucified God*.

119. Williams, *Arius: Heresy and Tradition* (2nd ed.), 235–36.

120. "The Barmen Declaration (May 1934)," in Lieth, ed., *Creeds of the Churches*, 520.

attempt by the theological apologists of apartheid to make race a God-given order of creation was a heresy that denied the Lordship of Christ over all reality.[121] Caesar's power and authority as well as that of the church can never be absolute, even if we brazenly confess "with our lips that Jesus is Lord."[122]

Both Barmen and Belhar stood on ground that had been prepared centuries before at Nicaea by Saint Athanasius, but they were anticipated by the earliest confession of faith recorded in the New Testament, namely that "Christ is Lord." This (unequivocal rejection of the absolute claims of both Caesar and pagan idolatry[123]) became the basis for membership of the WCC when it was founded in 1948—a commitment then explicitly expressed in Trinitarian terms in the WCC's statement on church unity adopted at New Delhi in 1961.[124]

Congregationalists do not normally recite the Nicene Creed in worship, but the doctrine of the Trinity is affirmed in countless statements of faith and sung in its hymns.[125] It is, after all, as P. T. Forsyth insisted, the belief that "makes Christianity Christian."[126] So, Congregationalists gladly give their assent to the ecumenical creeds.[127] But the original confession "Christ is Lord" remains the basis for church membership and, together with the words of Saint Paul that "the Lord is the Spirit, and where the Spirit of the Lord is, there is freedom,"[128] it expresses the core of its doctrine.

Acknowledging the "freedom of the Spirit" is critical if we are to understand, with Bonhoeffer, "who Christ is, for us, *today*"

---

121. See Templin, *Ideology on a Frontier*, 301; Bosch, "Nothing but a Heresy."

122. Rom 10:9; See de Gruchy, "Barmen: A Symbol of Contemporary Liberation."

123. Rom 10:9. See Moule, *Origin of Christology*, 35–45; Barrett, *Romans*, 200–201; Williams, *On Christian Theology*, 231.

124. See Leith, *Creeds of the Churches*, 583.

125. See, for example, "The Creed of 1883," in Walker, *Creeds and Platforms of Congregationalism*, 580; Manning, *Hymns of Wesley and Watts*.

126. Forsyth, *Faith, Freedom and the Future*, 263.

127. See Forsyth, *Congregationalism and Reunion*, 65–66.

128. 2 Cor 3:17.

in the changing historical contexts in which we live.[129] As he said, in addressing the need for the ecumenical church to confess its faith as Europe stood on the brink of war in 1932, the church must proclaim the Word of God not as a set of principles but concretely because "that which is 'always' true is precisely not true 'today': God is for us 'always' *God* precisely '*today*.'"[130]

The Nicene Creed, we should not forget was a response to a particular crisis in the ecumenical church in the fourth century, so while it remains a test of orthodoxy, it does not cover all the bases of Christian faith or stand apart from the Scriptures.[131] For example, it does not declare that "God is love," which, according to Saint Augustine, is what the doctrine of the Trinity is about.[132] Indeed, the fact that Christendom was torn apart in the eleventh century, and again by the Protestant Reformation in the sixteenth, despite a shared affirmation of the Nicene Creed, demonstrates that Christian unity requires more than subscription to a creed enforced by the princes of Christendom. The truth is, neither an infallible Bible nor an infallible pope, neither creeds nor confessions of faith have managed to hold the ecumenical church or even denominations together when threatened by cultural and social forces. And when political and ecclesiastical authority jointly combine to enforce uniformity, they undermine the integrity and witness of the church and provoke schism. That is why informed dissent is critical for the life and mission of the church in the world, and for safeguarding orthodoxy and orthopraxis.

G. K. Chesterton, a Roman Catholic, famously described orthodoxy as a "whirling adventure."[133] That might not be the language of Eastern Orthodoxy, but more soberly, as Kallistos Ware, one of its bishops, tells us, orthodoxy is always about more than ascribing to a statement of faith, a set of principles, or even biblical texts; it is a way of living in and traveling towards the mystery of

---

129. See de Gruchy, *Bonhoeffer's Questions*, 39–96.
130. Bonhoeffer, *Ecumenical, Academic, and Pastoral Work*, 359–60.
131. See Dodd, *Apostolic Preaching*.
132. 1 John 4:8. See Augustine, *Trinity*, 8.5 (pp. 251–55).
133. Chesterton, *Orthodoxy*, 100.

God.¹³⁴ And ever since, as a student in the United States, I listened to lectures by Alexander Schmemann, an émigré Russian Orthodox theologian, I have appreciated Eastern Orthodoxy for that reason.¹³⁵ I have also discovered that there are profound connections between Orthodoxy and Bonhoeffer's ecclesiology, spirituality, and understanding of nature and salvation.¹³⁶ So even if I am not Orthodox according to the strict norms of Eastern Orthodoxy, I believe I am, in Bernard Lord Manning's words, an "orthodox dissenter."¹³⁷

AN ECUMENICAL JUBILEE

Martin Luther's critique of papal triumphalism began after his disillusioning visit to Rome in 1510. Much had changed in the Catholic Church by the time Bonhoeffer visited Rome as a student in 1924. and more has changed since I visited Rome in 1964 when the Second Vatican Council was in session. But wars have not ceased, neither has poverty, injustice, or the onslaught of atavistic nationalism. And this is the context in which I end my discussion in Rome because it is there that Pope Francis (surely a preeminent dissenter of our time) declared 2025 a Jubilee Year of Hope.¹³⁸ In tandem, the World Council of Churches named 2025 "An Ecumenical Year on the Pilgrimage of Justice, Reconciliation, and Unity."¹³⁹

According to the Hebrew Bible, a Year of Jubilee was meant to be celebrated every fifty years in Israel by releasing people from the burden of their debts, setting slaves free, returning property to its

---

134. Ware, *Orthodox Way*.

135. See Schmemann, *For the Life of the World*. See de Gruchy, *Icons as a Means of Grace*.

136. Pelikan, *Spirit of Eastern Christendom*, 1–7.

137. Manning, *Essays in Orthodox Dissent*. Manning (1892–1942), a Congregational layman, taught medieval history at Cambridge University.

138. See Pope Francis, *Hope*.

139. As designated by the World Council of Churches, See *Nicaea2025@wcc-coe.org*.

rightful owners, and allowing the earth to lie fallow and to recover from producing crops.[140] It is unlikely that this ever happened, yet Jesus surely had it in mind when, according to Luke, he began his ministry in the synagogue in Nazareth by saying that he had been anointed by the Spirit to "proclaim the year of the Lord's favor," which was "good news to the poor, . . . release to the captives . . . , recovery of sight to the blind," and freedom for the oppressed.[141]

The Nicene Creed makes no reference to the prophetic ministry of Jesus, a subject that was not even discussed in the debates that preceded the Council of Nicaea.[142] Of course, Christians believe that Jesus is more than a prophet, but he clearly identified his mission with that of the Hebrew prophets of social justice, something that is confirmed throughout Luke's Gospel from Mary's Magnificat to the parable of Dives and Lazarus.[143] And the latter significantly concludes with Jesus saying that if people "do not listen to Moses and the prophets, neither will they be convinced even if someone rises from the dead."[144]

The prophetic witness of the church was pushed to the periphery of Christendom from the outset, and throughout subsequent history established authority has tried to silence the voice of dissent. Despite this, dissenters across the ecumenical spectrum have regularly arisen to bear witness to Christ by word and action. They have not been confined to any denomination or tradition, and some have stayed on the periphery of the church. As a Congregationalist, like the Lutheran Bonhoeffer, I belong first of all to the ecumenical church not least because Congregationalism was never meant to be a denomination; it became one by default. Nevertheless, I continue to remember my Congregational heritage that in South Africa goes back to John and Jane Philip, for whom being evangelical meant both trusting in God's saving grace alone and struggling for social justice, a heritage that was and remains

---

140. Lev 25:1–13.
141. Luke 4:16–21. See Isa 61:1–2. See also Pope Francis, *Hope*, 117–18.
142. See Dunn, *Christology in the Making*, 136–41.
143. See Burridge, *Imitating Jesus*, 234–82.
144. Luke 16:31.

ecumenical from the outset. And during 2025, the seventeen-hundredth anniversary year of the Council of Nicaea, I join with the millions of others in affirming its great ecumenical creed and listening to what the Spirit is saying to the church today as we are led more deeply into the truth in love and justice.

2

Happiness in a World at War

Those who mourn are those who are prepared to renounce and live without everything the world calls happiness and peace . . . They mourn over the world, its guilt, its fate, and its happiness.

—Bonhoeffer[1]

Who in our time could . . . lightheartedly make music, nurture friendship, play, and be happy? Certainly not the "ethical" person, but only the Christian.

—Bonhoeffer[2]

"Who, in our time, can be happy?" Bonhoeffer asked his niece Renate Bethge and her husband, Eberhard, in a letter from Tegel Military Prison. The world was at war; the Holocaust—as Bonhoeffer already knew—was in full swing; he was awaiting trial on

---

1. Bonhoeffer, *Discipleship*, 103–4.
2. Bonhoeffer, *Letters and Papers*, 268.

suspicion of helping Jews escape the gas chambers; he was separated from his fiancée, Maria; and he could hear the nightly bombing of Berlin, where his parents lived. How could anyone be happy at such a time? And what are we to make of his answer: "Certainly not the 'ethical' person, but only the Christian"? But who is this "'ethical' person" who cannot be happy, and who is "the Christian" who can? And how could Bonhoeffer consider himself "happy" when separated from family, fiancée, and friends, and contemplating suicide?[3] And, what about the newlyweds, Renate and Eberhard? How could they enjoy the pleasures of their life together with a good conscience at such a time, especially as Eberhard was about to leave for the Italian battle front as a conscripted soldier?[4]

How can anyone be happy, we may well ask, whether then or now, when there is so much violence and war, suffering and sorrow, in the world. And what has any of this to do with a possible conversation mooted by Rowan Williams between Bonhoeffer and Saint Peter Damien, an eleventh-century Italian austere contemplative and monastic reformer who was likened to Saint Francis Assisi and praised by Dante, but also a cardinal who advocated papal power? Yet, "in the desperate climate of this century," Williams suggests, "it may help us to go back to the [bleak] world that produced Cluny and Camaldoli" and ponder what Damien and Bonhoeffer might have said to one another.[5] My hunch is that they might have discussed what it means to be happy in bad times, or what it means to be a saint when everything is falling apart.

In the midst of the Church Struggle against Nazism several years before the beginning of the Second World War, Bonhoeffer was convinced that the truly happy are "those who are prepared to renounce and live without everything the world calls happiness and peace."[6] That would have resonated with Saint Damien. But I wonder how Damien would have reacted to what Bonhoeffer told

---

3. See Bonhoeffer, *Letters and Papers*, 70–74. 180, 567.

4. See Bethge's letter to Bonhoeffer, January 2nd, 1944, in Bonhoeffer, *Letters and Papers*, 248.

5. Williams, *Way of St Benedict*, 105.

6. Matt 5:14; Bonhoeffer, *Discipleship*, 103–4.

Bethge in a letter from prison. Recalling his friendship at Union Seminary with Jean Lasserre, a French Reformed pastor and pacifist who told him that his desire was to become a saint, Bonhoeffer said that he had only wanted to learn to live by faith. Then, later in life, he told Bethge, he discovered that this is only possible "by living fully in the midst of life's tasks, questions, successes and failures, experiences, and perplexities."[7]

While this difference between the saintly Lasserre and Damien on the one hand, and Bonhoeffer on the other, may reflect historic differences on the doctrine of sanctification, I do not think that they are that far apart unless saintliness is understood as a way of escape from worldly responsibility. But I think that the conversation between Bonhoeffer and Damien would have soon focused on how anyone could be "happy" at the same time as sharing in the "suffering of God in the world."[8] A question that troubles all who try to follow the way of Jesus as we daily witness the suffering of the victims of disease, hunger, and war, even if we do not experience it directly as it was, for example, by Saint Damien's nineteenth-century namesake, Saint Damien of Molokai, an island in Hawaii, who contracted leprosy while ministering to the needs of lepers.

The problem of theodicy, or how can we justify faith in a God of love in a world of so much suffering, has always been the main obstacle to faith in God. That it was foremost in Bonhoeffer's mind in prison is expressed in his poem "Christians and Heathen." There, he speaks of people standing "by God in God's own pain" as God suffers with and grieves for a world in pain.[9] But how does this correlate with us "being happy," if at all?

---

7. Bonhoeffer, *Letters and Papers*, 541–42
8. Bonhoeffer, *Letters and Papers*, 485–86.
9. Bonhoeffer, *Letters and Papers*, 461.

BEING HAPPY

There are two German words that are usually translated into English as "happy." The first, which is used in Bonhoeffer's question from prison, is *Freude*, that is happiness as joy or delight; the second is *Glück*, happiness as good fortune.[10] The same distinction, which has influenced moral philosophy ever since, was drawn by Aristotle, for whom true happiness is not the outcome of self-seeking pleasure but the fulfilment that results from doing what is virtuous, the outcome of a life well lived.[11] We can enjoy many things, such as playing games, but not all, says Aristotle, lead to a lasting happiness of soul.[12]

Eudaimonia ("happiness," or literally "living well") is not found in the New Testament, but *makarios* (blessed), its nearest equivalent, is often used, and this results from delighting in and doing the will of God. Saint Augustine, seeped in moral philosophy and the Bible, and reflecting on his own journey, tells us that the search for both happiness and fulfilment, derives from a divinely given desire for God, who is its source and goal.[13] He also tells us that we will often endure "evil circumstances" in achieving happiness, for "great joy is often preceded by great pain."[14]

There is, then, as Bonhoeffer observed in writing about the cost of discipleship, a fundamental difference between "what the world calls happiness" and the blessings that result from following Jesus.[15] But did this require giving up all worldly pleasures, including those associated with married life, as Saint Damien the monk did, though not Jean Lasserre, and as Bonhoeffer as a young theologian thought he should do?[16] Or did it only require

10. See Bonhoeffer's prison poem "Glück und Unglück" translated as "Fortune and Calamity," in *Letters and Papers*, 431–42.
11. Aristotle, *Ethics of Aristotle*, 35–52; bk. 1 chs. 2–13.
12. See MacIntyre, *After Virtue*, 150–51.
13. Bonhoeffer, *Letters and Papers*, 52; Augustine, *Trinity*, 1/18, 77.
14. Augustine, *Trinity*, 349; see Augustine, *Confessions*, IV/5/10; VIII/3/8; X/10/29; X/21/31.
15. Bonhoeffer, *Discipleship*, 105.
16. Bonhoeffer, *Discipleship*, 104.

giving up those pleasures associated with a carefree, self-centered aestheticism such as Søren Kierkegaard turned his back on when he opted to follow Christ?

Bonhoeffer learned much about the "cost of discipleship" from Kierkegaard, who, as he reminds us, was also responsible for the banishment of "aesthetic existence" from the church.[17] But whereas for Kirkegaard "aesthetic existence" was understood as a self-centered, pleasure-seeking aestheticism, Bonhoeffer had come to the conclusion that properly understood, "aesthetic existence" was essential to being truly human, being a Christian, and being "happy." If that is so, then "aesthetic existence" should surely not be banished from the church but renewed within it. Indeed, could it not be, as I shall argue in the next chapter, that the recovery of "aesthetic existence" in the church today is fundamental in responding to the challenge of artificial general intelligenced?

Bonhoeffer's comment on "aesthetic existence" in his letter to the Bethges from prison was not only a passing thought, even though he only mentions it this once. The fact is, "aesthetic existence" was embodied in his life, and permeates much else that he talked about in his prison letters.[18] It is certainly implied when he tells Bethge that only if "we hold fast to Christ as *cantus firmus*" will we "discover the polyphony of life, that is, life in all its fullness."[19] For only where Christ "the *cantus firmus* is clear and plain," can the counterpoint "be developed to its limits."[20] In following Christ, then, we are led "into many different dimensions of life at the same time; in a way we accommodate God and the whole world within us."[21] To be fully human in Christ is living life polyphonically or "more abundantly."[22] And, surely, that is happiness!

---

17. See Bonhoeffer, *Discipleship*, 7–12; Balthasar, *Seeing the Form*, XIII.9, 45–57.

18. See de Gruchy, *Christianity, Art, and Transformation*, 138–47.

19. Bonhoeffer, *Letters and Papers*, 394; Pangritz, *Polyphony of Life*, 52–64.

20. Bonhoeffer, *Letters and Papers*, 303.

21. Bonhoeffer, *Letters and Papers*, 405.

22. Cf. John 10:10

Given that Bonhoeffer's Christology always has ecclesiological consequences, it follows that this Christocentric understanding of "aesthetic existence" must in some way relate to the church, which for Bonhoeffer is "Christ existing as a community of persons."[23] Indeed, if "aesthetic existence" is understood from a social and ecclesial perspective, it cannot be confused with self-centered individualism or self-seeking "aestheticism." On the contrary, it must embrace "the other" and so bring personal fulfilment and happiness to all. As such, "aesthetic existence" is of the *essence* of the church and not just its *bene esse*, and this requires, as Bonhoeffer says, that the church be a "sphere of freedom." But sadly, this was not how Bonhoeffer, his family, or his colleagues in the Resistance experienced the church. That was one reason why he was astounded when during the Third Reich, some secular humanists became friends with confessing Christians in the struggle against tyranny.[24]

BEING A CHRISTIAN HUMANIST

Growing up, Bonhoeffer was nurtured in a humanist environment.[25] To pursue his calling to become a pastor he had to convince his father, a renowned scientist, that he was not wasting his talents.[26] Then, as a young theologian under the sway of Barth, who had yet to affirm the "humanity of God,"[27] he had to come to terms with the anti-Barthian critique of his liberal teacher, Harnack.[28] This personal struggle took on a new dynamic when, as an ardent "Barthian," Bonhoeffer went to study at Union Theological Seminary in New York (1930–1931) where he was challenged

23. Bonhoeffer, *Sanctorum Communio*, 127–34.
24. See Bethge, "Bonhoeffer's Theology of Friendship."
25. De Gruchy, "Dietrich Bonhoeffer as Christian Humanist." See Zimmermann, *Incarnational Humanism*, esp. 309–20.
26. See de Gruchy, "Dietrich Bonhoeffer as Christian Humanist."
27. See Barth, *Humanity of God*.
28. See Barth, *Theological Existence Today!*; Rumscheidt, *Revelation and Theology*.

by Reinhold Niebuhr and others to connect his dogmatic theology to social ethical responsibility. It was also there that he made life-changing friendships with two fellow students, Jean Lasserre, whom we have already met, and Frank Fisher an African American.

Fisher introduced Bonhoeffer to the Harlem Renaissance and so helped him appreciate the history of slavery and the continuing plight of African Americans as they struggled against racism.[29] Fisher also introduced Bonhoeffer to the Abyssinian Church in Harlem where Bonhoeffer experienced the church as a vibrant mix of evangelical passion, a spirituality expressed in songs that arose out of the struggle against slavery, and a socially concerned community. All of this gave fresh life to Bonhoeffer's somewhat academic ecclesiology and shifted his perspective on life from being bourgeois Eurocentric to one we now call postcolonial.[30]

On his return to Germany, Bonhoeffer became involved in the life of the Confessing Church and the ecumenical movement in its peacemaking endeavors. Then for a year and a half he was the pastor of two German-speaking Lutheran congregations in London (1933–1935). After that brief sojourn, he went back to Germany where he became director of the Confessing Church seminary at Finkenwalde in 1935. It was there that he wrote *Discipleship* and gathered some of his students together into the intentional Community of Brethren, which he later described in *Life Together*.[31] One of these students was Bethge, who soon became his closest confidant and, in due course, his "confessor."[32]

When, during 1940, the seminary was declared illegal by the Gestapo and forced underground, and Bonhoeffer himself was banned from teaching and preaching, he became involved in the Resistance. He then began work on his *Ethics* and, sometime in 1942 while writing at the Benedictine monastery at Ettal in Bavaria, he recorded "one of the most astounding experiences" he

---

29. Williams, *Bonhoeffer's Black Jesus*.

30. See Young, *No Difference in the Fare*, 21–27; de Gruchy, *Faith Facing Reality*, 42–55.

31. Bonhoeffer, "Life Together"; "Prayerbook of the Bible."

32. See Bonhoeffer, *Letters and Papers*, 181, 200

had had "during the years of trial for all that was Christian."[33] Whereas until recent times reason, culture, humanity, tolerance and autonomy, all virtues and values of secular humanism, had "served as battle cries against the church, against Christianity, even against Jesus Christ," they had now "surprisingly found themselves in very close proximity to the Christian domain."[34] Bonhoeffer had in mind how some members of his own family circle, such as his brother-in-law Hans von Dohnanyi, who had brought him into the Resistance, and a handful of other friends who had previously had little time for the church now found common cause with those Christians who courageously opposed Nazism.[35]

The reality was that since the eighteenth century, these two worlds had drifted apart despite the attempt by luminaries of liberal Protestantism from Schleiermacher to Harnack to bridge the gap. But now, paradoxically, just when, under the influence of Barth, the Confessing Church became more theologically dogmatic, something remarkable happened. For it was then, writes Bonhoeffer, when "the exclusive demand for an unequivocal confession of Christ caused" a "band of confessing Christians to become smaller and smaller" that Jesus's exclusive saying "whoever is not for me is against me" became an experience of inclusive protection to "wounded justice, oppressed truth, humiliated humanity" and "violated freedom." Moreover, these humanist concerns found in "the Christian community, or rather its Lord, Jesus Christ," demonstrated the truth of "the other saying of Jesus: 'Whoever is not against us is with us.'"[36] In other words, the more faithful its confession of Christ became against National Socialism, the more the Confessing Church demonstrated the relevance of the gospel to the struggle for human freedom, dignity, and well-being, without necessarily recognizing the connection. This is a remarkable example of how Christian dissent has served the mission of the

---

33. Bonhoeffer, *Ethics*, 339.
34. Bonhoeffer, *Ethics*, 340.
35. See Sifton and Stern, *No Ordinary Men*.
36. Bonhoeffer, *Ethics*, 343–44.

church when the church itself has succumbed to political power and compromised its mission.

Bonhoeffer's experience later resonated with those of us who were engaged in the Church Struggle against apartheid in South Africa. We, too, found common cause with many concerned humanists, some of them also lapsed Christians, as well as with people of other faith traditions, or of no faith commitment. This solidarity may have been regarded by some as only strategic and pragmatic, but Bonhoeffer understood it at a deeper level. For him it was based on values that have *Christian* roots even if this was not acknowledged by all Christians or by those heirs of the Enlightenment who, like his friends in the Resistance, found "themselves in very close proximity to the Christian domain."[37]

For Bonhoeffer, this surprising turn of events was not a reason for Christian triumphalism because for them the church of Christendom had failed and remained a problem. What actually attracted them, Bonhoeffer said, was not the church but Christ, who, as the representative of humanity, had taken form in the world in a handful of friends struggling against evil.[38] Together, they had learned to "see things from below" and discovered "that personal suffering is a more useful key . . . than personal happiness (*Glück*) for exploring the meaning of the world in contemplation and action."[39]

But if it was this christological perspective, "grounded beyond what is below and above" that enabled them "to do justice to life in all its dimensions," why does Bonhoeffer say that those humanists who shared that perspective were only in "close proximity" to Christian faith? One reason is that he did not want to claim triumphantly that they had become Christian without their consent. A more profound reason is that Bonhoeffer's understanding of humanism was grounded in transcendent reality and specifically in his Christology. As such it was more than epistemological,[40]

---

37. Bonhoeffer, *Ethics*, 340.
38. See Bonhoeffer, "Lecture Course: The Nature of the Church," 296–98.
39. Bonhoeffer, *Letters and Papers*, 52.
40. Bonhoeffer, *Act and Being*, 39.

more than what Kierkegaard referred to as the "vaporized humanism," or what Charles Taylor calls the "exclusive humanism" of modernity.[41] Bonhoeffer's humanism was inclusive because it was incarnational—or as he put it, "our relationship to God is no religious relationship to some highest, most powerful, and best being imaginable" but a "new life in 'being there for others,' through participation in the being of Jesus." From this perspective

> the transcendent is . . . the neighbor within reach in any given situation. God in human form! . . . the human being for others! That is, the Crucified One. The human being living out of the transcendent.[42]

The implication of this is that we cannot "do justice to life in all its dimensions" and find happiness by grasping for power and wealth or abusing others, but only by standing in solidarity with them, especially those who suffer.[43]

But if we do express such solidarity, Bonhoeffer asked himself as he asks us, is it possible to be happy at the same time with a clear conscience? Indeed, can sadness coexist with happiness and even deepen our understanding and experience of both? To be more specific, with the newly married Bethges in mind, could Christians enjoy the pleasures of married life and physical love (*eros*) at the same time as seeking to love (*agape*) God and others in the middle of war and devastation? Are not "costly discipleship" and "aesthetic existence" mutually exclusive as was implied in Bonhoeffer's book *Discipleship*, which he wrote while still contemplating a life of celibacy in the service of Christ?

But now, in prison, Bonhoeffer began to express reservations about what he had previously written about the cost of discipleship. This prompted him to write his first expressly called theological letter to Bethge (July 21, 1944) from prison.[44] "In the last few

---

41. Taylor, *Secular Age*, 221–69, 539–72; Kierkegaard, *Journals*, 209.
42. Bonhoeffer, *Letters and Papers*, 501. See de Gruchy, "Dietrich Bonhoeffer as Christian Humanist."
43. See de Gruchy, *Faith Facing Reality*, 56–78.
44. Bonhoeffer, *Letters and Papers*, 485–86.

years" he wrote, "I have come to know and understand more and more the profound this-worldliness of Christianity." But he hastened to add that by this he "did not mean the shallow and banal this-worldliness of the enlightened, the bustling, the comfortable, or the lascivious, but the profound this-worldliness that shows discipline and includes the ever-present knowledge of death and resurrection."[45] In other words, whatever he meant by "aesthetic existence," he did not intend to dilute discipleship or cheapen the Beatitudes. On the contrary, he tells us, he still stood by what he had written in *Discipleship* but could now see its danger.

The danger was that of always being *against* the world rather than embracing it in both its joys and sorrows and living life in "all its dimensions."[46] Instead of being at the mercy of self-centered passions, whether of aestheticism *or* morbid asceticism, in embracing the world in this way we become open to God's passion for the world, and begin, as Kierkegaard describes it, to "live poetically."[47] This means, in Ingolf Dalferth's words, becoming free "to see, form and shape" life in "relationship with God as an original love relationship," and, in the process, developing the ability to use personal freedom "in unexpected and surprising ways" by "seeing, imagining, dreaming, acting, loving together with others in a joint effort of boundless humanity and *Mitmenschlichkeit*."[48] For that reason it had become necessary to renew "aesthetic existence" in the church as a "sphere of freedom."

THE CHURCH AS A "SPHERE OF FREEDOM"

While much of Bonhoeffer's "Outline for a Book" drafted in prison provides a brief analysis of the "world come of age" and his theological response, his main concern was its *ecclesiological*

---

45. Bonhoeffer, *Letters and Papers*, 485.
46. Bonhoeffer, *Letters and Papers*, 485–86.
47. See Walsh, *Living Poetically*.
48. Dalferth, *Passion of Possibility*, 253–54.

consequences.[49] For if Christ is the "human being who exists for others," then the church can only be the church if it does the same. But how does the church retain its Christian identity if it becomes immersed in the life of the world? Drawing on his experience of Benedictine monastic life and the Community of Brothers he formed at Finkenwalde, Bonhoeffer advocates practicing a monastic-like *disciplina arcanum* or "hidden discipline" as a counterpoint to worldly involvement.[50] This involved communal worship, practicing the *lectio divina*, and celebrating the mysteries of faith. In coming to this conclusion Bonhoeffer was in unison with Kierkegaard's conviction about the need to dissent from Christendom in Denmark and return to "the monastery from which Luther broke away."[51]

It is surely remarkable that Bonhoeffer draws inspiration from monasticism in seeking a model for the renewal of the church in the secular, modern world. And yet attempts to reform monasticism in the Middle Ages, such as those initiated by Saint Bernard of Clairvaux and Saint Romuald of Camaldoli, were not only focused on the interior life of the monastery but on how it should relate to the world, which later became the major concern of Thomas Merton in more recent times. If this is so, then I am sure that Rowan Williams's hypothetical conversation between Bonhoeffer and Saint Damien, a Camaldolesen monk, would not have been about *whether* but *how* Christians should be engaged in the life of the world.

Undoubtedly, as Bonhoeffer said in a sermon prepared in prison for the baptism of Dietrich Bethge in May 1944, the church would need to be prophetic and "speak the word of God in such a way that the world is changed and renewed." This, he said, would require "a new language, perhaps quite nonreligious language," one that is "liberating and redeeming like Jesus's language," a language that spoke of "a new righteousness and truth . . . proclaiming

---

49. Bonhoeffer, *Letters and Papers*, 503–4.
50. Bonhoeffer, *Letters and Papers*, 373; See de Gruchy, *This Monastic Moment*, 168–69.
51. Kierkegaard, *Journals*, 240; de Gruchy, *This Monastic Moment*, 118–20.

that God makes peace with humankind and that God's kingdom is drawing near."[52] But this required more than a change in language and preaching style.[53] It had to do with the *way* in which the church existed in the world, namely not being preoccupied with its own self-preservation, but being focused on the need of the world. That is why Bonhoeffer says that "we can be Christians today in only two ways, through prayer and in doing justice among human beings," for all "Christian thinking, talking, and organizing must be born anew, out of that prayer and action."[54]

Soon after he prepared this baptismal sermon his fiancée, Maria, visited Bonhoeffer in prison for the first time. Then, unexpectedly, he began to write poetry. Unsurprisingly, his first poem, "The Past," was an expression of romantic love, and his second was about happiness—"Glück und Unglück," good fortune in contrast to calamity.[55] For, uppermost in Bonhoeffer's mind must have been his hope that he and Maria would still get married, and that their love for each other would be fulfilled in happiness, even though the odds of that happening were diminishing with the passing of each day.

The significance of Bonhoeffer's turn to poetry was, however, more than an expression of his existential longing; it was complementary to his theological explorations, that is, with his attempt to find the new language with which to express faith. As Bernd Wannenwetsch says, the apophatic nature of poetic language was "a particularly appropriate medium to capture the complexity of Bonhoeffer's theological thought" in prison.[56] And, as his poems suggest, this includes, not least, his passing comment on the renewal of "aesthetic existence" in the church as a "sphere of freedom." Coupled to this was his doubt as to whether a person "who doesn't know anything of this sphere of freedom can be a good parent, citizen, and worker, and also be a Christian," and therefore

---

52. Bonhoeffer, *Letters and Papers*, 390.
53. See Bonhoeffer, *Letters and Papers*, 372.
54. Bonhoeffer, *Letters and Papers*, 389,
55. Bonhoeffer, *Letters and Papers*, 418–21, 441–42.
56. Wannenwetsch, ed., *Who Am I?*, 4.

"be happy."[57] But how could the church be renewed as a "sphere of freedom" in which this could happen?

What Bonhoeffer proposes might momentarily suggest that he had the historic Free Churches (Baptist, Congregational, Methodist) as distinct from the established German *Landeskirche* in mind.[58] But for Bonhoeffer, the freedom of the church was not something granted by the state as, for example, in the passing of the Voluntary Act in the Cape Parliament with which I began this book, but the freedom of the church as God's gift to the church that had to be embraced and expressed irrespective of cultural or political restraint.[59] In other words, it was not primarily about the freedom of the church from state control, but the freedom of the church to be the church. It was none other than the liberty of the Spirit about which Saint Paul wrote to the churches in Galatia: "For freedom Christ has set us free. Stand firm, therefore, and do not submit again to a yoke of slavery."[60]

The "yoke of slavery" to which Paul here refers was both the pagan practices demanded by Hellenistic and Roman civic authorities, and the legalistic constraints that the Judaizing faction in the church insisted should be observed by Gentile converts.[61] Jesus offered them freedom from both though not a license to do as they pleased.[62] And given the fact that the churches in Galatia would have included ex-slaves, Paul's words spoke directly to their experience. This would have also resonated with the descendants of slaves Bonhoeffer met at the Abyssinian Baptist Church in Harlem, who still suffered from endemic racism, much like those ministered to by John and Jane Philip in Cape Town in the early nineteenth century and their descendants under apartheid.[63]

57. Bonhoeffer, *Letters and Papers*, 268.

58. See Bonhoeffer, *Letters and Papers*, 503.

59. See Clements, "Freedom of the Church."

60. Gal 5:1. On the importance of this text for the development of the Nicene doctrine of Trinity, see Hill, Introduction, 35.

61. See Longenecker, *Galatians*, 223–25.

62. Williams, *On Christian Theology*, 231.

63. See Bonhoeffer's "Essay about American Protestantism," 456–58.

But in writing to Bethge, Bonhoeffer also had in mind that while the medieval church had been a "sphere of freedom" in which Christianity and classical culture creatively combined to produce Renaissance humanism, that freedom had been squandered.[64] As a result, the fruitful interaction that had so enriched the life of Christendom had been overtaken by inquisitions, crusades, polemic, intolerance, division, and interminable wars of religion. This had led to the alienation of humanism from the church during the Enlightenment as well as ecclesiastical resistance to scientific advancement and aesthetic creativity. As a result, an increasingly secular world had replaced the church as a "sphere of freedom"; science had taken control of knowledge, and art had claimed its own autonomy.

This left the church, both Catholic and Protestant, to be the moral guardian of private and public life. This was certainly true of the Church of the Union (Lutheran and Reformed), the *Evangelische Landeskirche* in Berlin-Brandenburg to which both Bonhoeffer and Bethge belonged. As a result the Prussian Protestant world was "so strongly defined by the four mandates"—marriage and family life, work, church, and state—"that the whole sphere of freedom" had "been pushed into the background."[65] The same happened most obviously, though not only, within the DRC in South Africa during the apartheid era. Church discipline ensured social and cultural conformity, thereby excluding and sometimes punishing dissent as happened to Beyers Naudé, as we have already noted.

In his *Ethics*, Bonhoeffer had previously written at length about the "four mandates" which provided society with clearly defined rules and boundaries that determined virtually every dimension of life.[66] The result was that many Christians lived by cast-iron principles rather than by exercising the freedom of responsibility, just as in South Africa there were many people of high moral principles who supported apartheid. Such people are represented

---

64. See Bonhoeffer, *Letters and Papers*, 268; Bonhoeffer, *Ethics*, 103–33; Zimmermann, *Incarnational Humanism*, 114–62.

65. Bonhoeffer, *Letters and Papers*, 268.

66. Bonhoeffer, *Ethics*, 18 et al.

by Bonhoeffer's "ethical person," whose moral principles, however worthy, are used to avoid necessary action.[67] By way of contrast to "the Christian," such people, says Bonhoeffer, could certainly not be happy! Nowhere is this better illustrated than in Jesus's parable of the good Samaritan where the priest and the Levite, who live by the letter of the law, are contrasted with the Samaritan, who disregards the rules of conventional religion to show compassion.[68]

Jesus does not question the high moral principles and purpose of the Pharisees, but he does present a radically different basis for ethical life, life defined by the liberating reign of God. In this "new world," says Bonhoeffer, there "is nothing problematic, tortured, or dark about the living and acting of human beings, but instead something self-evident, joyous, certain, and clear."[69] Moreover, this "new world" is not only a future possibility; it is meant to be embodied in the church as a "sphere of freedom" that "exists for others," and within which people discover "life in all its dimensions possible." As Bonhoeffer wrote in his discussion of Christian formation in his *Ethics*: "The church is nothing but that piece of humanity where Christ really has taken form . . . Therefore essentially its first concern is not with the so-called religious functions of human beings, but with the existence in the world of whole human beings in all their relationships."[70]

If this is so, then it follows that the "church must participate in the worldly tasks of life in the community—not dominating but helping and serving"—that is, showing what it means "to be there for others," especially for the poor. To do so, the church "will have to confront the vices of hubris, the worship of power."[71] Indeed, only in this way can the church be renewed and become a "sphere of freedom" in which "aesthetic existence" is possible, fostered by art, play, and friendship within the church.

---

67. Bonhoeffer, *Letters and Papers*, 39; see also Bethge, "Bonhoeffer's Theology of Friendship," 96.

68. Luke 10:25–37.

69. Bonhoeffer, *Ethics*, 309.

70. Bonhoeffer, *Ethics*, 97

71. Bonhoeffer, *Letters and Papers*, 503–4.

NURTURING AESTHETIC EXISTENCE

Bonhoeffer was a well-trained pianist with a remarkable knowledge of the visual arts. He knew that through art we hear and see the world differently, and as a result, our lives become more fully human.[72] As Bernard Lonergan observes, art "makes ordinary human life more than biological, artistic, or intellectual," because it fosters creativity, which leads to the embodiment of "faith, beauty, and the admirable" in our lives and actions even "before it is given a still freer realization in painting and sculpture, in music and poetry."[73] In the process, faith discerns the creator Spirit awakening the conviction that there is, in Jeremy Begbie's words, "more to the world than we will ever be able to account for, more than could ever be fully discovered, thought, or spoken."[74]

None of this excludes the need for aesthetic judgment; rather we recognize that by stimulating imagination and nurturing creativity, the arts help us become more truly human in an increasingly reductionist and cybertechnical world. Moreover, through the Spirit the arts not only become a means of grace and a source of joy and delight, but they awaken us to the painful realities of human suffering and ecological decay by suggesting alternative ways to envisage the future and possibilities for action. We may be able to live without pleasure, but we cannot live without embracing God's gift of the happiness. This is an act of defiance against suffering not its denial.[75]

The fact that Bonhoeffer speaks of "play" in the same breath as "art" is not accidental. Play has long been included in aesthetic theory as a way of knowing ourselves and the world better. It was also an important aspect of Bonhoeffer's life. As Charles Marsh tells us, Bonhoeffer played tennis, danced and skied with as much

---

72. See Gadamer, *Truth and Method*, 89; see also Pangritz, *Polyphony of Life*.

73. Lonergan, *Insight*, 187.

74. Begbie *Abundantly More*, 177.

75. Gilbert, "Brief for the Defense," 317.

vigor as he played the piano.[76] Marsh also reports that while visiting the Community of the Resurrection at Mirfield during his stay in England, Bonhoeffer "seemed as thrilled by the sight of Anglican monks enjoying sport—tennis, soccer, cricket, even rugby—in the afternoon as by the solemnities of compline and the simplicity of communal life."[77] To be sure, play can also subvert our ability to face reality and address social challenges, thereby becoming a way of escaping reality and a commercial enterprise that reinforces our dehumanizing instincts.[78] Or, as Neil Postman graphically puts it, through excessive play, we can even "amuse ourselves to death."[79] But the play to which Bonhoeffer refers is a way whereby we affirm our common humanity and build more humane communities.

While art and play are key elements in describing and nurturing "aesthetic existence," Bonhoeffer's focus in writing to Bethge was especially on the role of friendship, mindful as they both were of the importance of their friendship in facing the realities of their time.[80] But of course, as Bethge documents, Bonhoeffer had developed significant friendships long before the two of them met at Finkenwalde. And the formation of trustworthy friendships during the years of the Church Struggle, as Bonhoeffer's with Franz Hildebrandt in the early days of the Church Struggle and with Hans von Dohnanyi in the Resistance, was critical. But his friendship with Bethge was exceptional, and never better expressed than when Bethge sang Franz Schubert's *Lieder* to Bonhoeffer's accompaniment on the piano.

But for Bonhoeffer, such friendship also belonged within the scope of Christian freedom and was fundamental to the life of the church. That is why "we must defend it confidently against all 'ethical' existences that may frown upon it—certainly without claiming for it the '*necessitas*' of a divine command, but by claiming the

---

76. Marsh, *Strange Glory*, 18.
77. Marsh, *Strange Glory*, 218.
78. Gadamer, "Play of Art," 130.
79. Postman, *Amusing Ourselves to Death*.
80. See Bethge, "Bonhoeffer's Theology of Friendship"; de Gruchy, *Daring, Trusting Spirit*, 79–86.

'*necessitas*' of *freedom*!"[81] "Unlike marriage and family relationships," Bonhoeffer continues, "friendship does not enjoy "recognized rights" proscribed by law, but "depends entirely on its own inherent quality." "As such it belongs to "the sphere of freedom [*Spielraum*]."[82] Within this realm, friendship, writes Bonhoeffer in a poem for Bethge, "is by far the rarest . . . and the most precious good . . . like the cornflowers belong to the field of grain."[83] It is surely for this reason that Jesus refers to his disciples as his "friends," and tells them that there is no greater love than that which is shown in laying down one's life for a friend.[84] As Jürgen Moltmann once described it, the church is meant to be "a fellowship of friends," journeying together into the love of the triune God as envisaged by Saint Augustine.[85]

In thinking about the role of friendship in the life of the church in a world on the brink of war, Bonhoeffer would undoubtedly have recalled his involvement in the World Alliance for Promoting Friendship Through the Churches of which he became the German Youth secretary at its founding Cambridge conference in 1930.[86] In a world at war, when spheres of freedom across national, ethnic, and religious boundaries are undermined by propaganda, censorship, and the instruments of "state security," friendships become critical for the peacemaking process that must inevitably begin. But they also give substance to Bonhoeffer's rhetorical question: "Who in our time can be happy?" Not the "'ethical' person," whose response is governed by moral precepts and principles that prevent action, but only the "Christian," who, in solidarity with others, prays and acts in the responsible freedom of the Spirit and makes lasting friendships.

---

81. Bonhoeffer, *Letters and Papers*, 268–300.

82. Bonhoeffer, *Letters and Papers*, 291.

83. Bonhoeffer, *Letters and Papers*. 268–69; de Gruchy, *Daring, Trusting Spirit*, 59–73.

84. John 15:13. See "φϊλός" in Stählin, "Φιλέω . . ." 159–64.

85. See Moltmann, *Church in the Power of the Spirit*, 314–17; see Burt, *Friendship and Society*, 55–59.

86. See Bethge, *Dietrich Bonhoeffer*, 238–48.

Going Against the Stream
WHAT, THEN, DOES HAPPINESS MEAN?

Bonhoeffer's reflections on happiness and "aesthetic existence" were evoked by the marriage of Renate and Eberhard Bethge to whom he wrote the letter with which I began this chapter. While he was delighted by their marriage, he was bothered about how it would affect their friendship going forward. To complicate matters further, Bonhoeffer had become engaged to Maria, much to the surprise of all who knew him. After all, she was only nineteen, making him twenty years her senior, and to most acquaintances and members of his family Dietrich was a confirmed bachelor. This would no doubt have pleased Kierkegaard, who thought that Lutheran pastors like Catholic priests should remain celibate. This conviction played a role in his ending his engagement to Regine Olsen and made him even more melancholic than he is generally thought to have been.[87]

But Bonhoeffer's hopes of marriage to Maria began to fade when, after the failure of the July 20th, 1944, plot on Hitler's life, he became resigned to his fate. Indeed, on December 19th, in anticipation of that probability, he sent a Christmas letter to Maria that he asked her to share with his parents and siblings. And, in thanking her for a letter he had received from her with its "kind thoughts, passages from the Bible, long forgotten conversations, pieces of music, books" all "invested with life and reality," he told her that he was now living "in a great unseen realm of whose real existence I'm in no doubt." Then, in virtually his last words to her Bonhoeffer spoke of *Glück* and *Freuden*, as though in the same breath:

> you mustn't think I am unhappy. Anyway, what do happiness (*glücklich*) and unhappiness (*unglücklich*) mean? They depend so little on circumstances and so much more on what goes on inside us. I'm thankful every day to have you—you and all of you—and that makes me happy (*glücklich*) and cheerful (*froh*).[88]

---

87. See Lowrie, *Kierkegaard*, 487–90.
88. Bonhoeffer and von Wedemeyer, *Love Letters from Cell 92*, 227–28.

3

Being Human in a Robotic World

The prototype from which the human form takes its shape is either the imaginative form of God based on human projection, or it is the true and living form of God which molds the human form into the image of God.

—Bonhoeffer[1]

It is for humankind to decide whether to become food for algorithms or to move forward on its own path, keeping its distinctive character and recovering that which is more important than necessary, the nucleus of every human being, their most intimate center, which is the heart.

—Pope Francis[2]

---

1. Bonhoeffer, *Discipleship*, 282–83.
2. Pope Francis, *Hope*, 281.

Going Against the Stream

In his autobiography, the late Pope Francis spoke about the promising role of artificial intelligence (AI) in creating "a new social system characterized by complex epoch-making transformations." He also warned of the danger of becoming so dependent on AI that we lose our souls, "the nucleus of every human being."[3] Today we find ourselves living with this tension between great promise and fearful danger. It is exhilarating and scary at the same time to be daily informed about the advances in cybertechnology and receiving computer program updates. Even as I write I have been informed online that OpenAI has released two open-language models that excel in advanced reasoning that can run on my laptop.

The aim of artificial general intelligence (AGI), says Douglas Hofstadter, a cognitive scientist, is "to get at what is happening when one's mind silently and invisibly chooses, from a myriad of alternatives, which one makes most sense in a very complex situation." This has become necessary, Hofstadter says, because there are "just too many things to take into account simultaneously for reasoning alone to be sufficient."[4] But AGI is not only intelligent, it is all-pervasive and producing robots with capabilities that exceed our own cognitive abilities. This raises fundamental questions about what it means to be human, what we mean by human consciousness and natural intelligence, and whether there are ethical boundaries to the enhancement of human life. Is "the essence of being human" expressed in "our ability to reach beyond our limitations," or is it to acknowledge them and respect our humanity?[5]

These are urgent concerns, for, as Yuval Noah Harari warns, we "don't know for how long we still have the power to shape these new realities."[6] In fact, says Toby Ord, an AGI guru, we face an

---

3. Pope Francis, *Hope*, 281.

4. Hofstadter, *Gödel, Escher, Bach*, 560; Dorobantu, "Artificial Intelligence and Christianity," 88; the development of AI and AGI is told in Olson, *Supremacy*.

5. See Delio, "Transhumanism and Transcendence," 146.

6. Harari, *Nexus*, 219.

irreversible "existential catastrophe,"[7] described by the cofounder of DeepMind, as "a tidal wave of powerful and rapidly growing technologies that have enormous potential to help us save the planet and promote global prosperity, but [are] equally able to destroy the world."[8] How then can AGI be controlled so that it serves rather than threatens both the common and our own personal good? And how should the church respond to the challenge, which we cannot wish away any more than some early Christian monks wished that Christendom would disappear?

FACING AN APPROACHING TSUNAMI

There was a huge time gap between the moment when humans learned to make fire and when we invented the microwave, and then in virtually no time at all we split the atom. So, too, my first computer, bought in 1983, was a processor of words that helped me write several books and prepared me to use more sophisticated machines before it became obsolete. Now the power of my present computer exceeds those that monitored the launching of Sputnik in 1957. Throughout this progression I have felt reasonably in control of the technology on my desk. No longer. The generative power of AGI is so awesome that its own pioneers fear it cannot be kept in check. The lifespan of computers may be limited, but the development of AGI is irreversible because it has reached "technological singularity," that is, the hypothetical point when growth becomes progressively uncontrollable.

As I reflect on this rapidly approaching cyber tsunami, the image of our technologically advanced civilization disappearing beneath the waves, like Plato's mythical Atlantis, flashes through my mind, as does the biblical myth of the collapse of the Tower of Babel. After all, it is the same human hubris that led to those ancient legendary and some real catastrophes that now drives us towards a dystopian graveyard.

---

7. Ord, *Precipice*.
8. Suleyman and Bhaskar, *Coming Wave*, 3.

Within this sobering global framework, the situation in the developing world has its own challenges.[9] There is, on the one hand, the naïve belief, globally shared, that AGI will save us in some miraculous way while, on the other, an inherent suspicion that AGI will perpetuate the exploitation of former colonies by controlling resources more efficiently. Adjunct to this cybernetic neocolonialism is the rapid and extensive "data colonization" of the world which serves to benefit a powerful few while increasing the oppression of the powerless many. It is not a coincidence that democracies are struggling to survive while cybernetic technology takes center stage as the instrument of choice for all in control.

The development of AGI has increased so much that some of its "owners" are now so wealthy that they can control governments, influence global politics, fund wars, and sponsor the exploration of space in cosmic-sized acts of hubris. In fact, AGI has become the perfect tool for dictators and despots who want to crush dissenters, as well as for unscrupulous sales representatives or televangelists who want to capture the market or save our souls for personal profit. Bonhoeffer described such as the "tyrannical despisers" of humanity" who praise themselves "before the masses ... with repulsive vanity while despising their rights."[10] The sobering reality is that "as long as commercial and political incentives are the guiding hand in AI development, we risk letting machines (and their human creators) off the hook for the choices they make on behalf of society."[11]

Furthermore, just as colonialism, commercial interest, and modernity are historically linked to mainstream Christian missions in Africa and elsewhere,[12] so today the growth of mega prosperity churches who support right-wing Christian nationalism is

---

9. Mokoena, "Holistic Ubuntu Artificial Intelligence Ethics Approach," based on Mokoena, "Towards an Ubuntu/Botho Ethics of Technology"; and Awasthi and Achar, "African Christian Theology in the Age of AI."

10. Bonhoeffer, *Ethics*, 73

11. Mubeen, *Mathematical Intelligence*, 269.

12. Comaroff and Comaroff, *Of Revelation and Revolution*, vol. 2, *Dialectics of Modernity*.

linked to their adeptness at using cybernetic technology.[13] As Beth Singler writes, the resurgence of Christian fundamentalism and its alignment with the political right cannot be dismissed as "the domain of the uneducated," for it is clearly connected to AI and technological savviness.[14] This applies equally to any ideologically driven perversion of religion. AGI also, inter alia, threatens education. It can, for example, inhibit creative thought and writing as well as critical thinking, to mention but two of many concerns. But irrespective of what we do, we are unlikely to stop teachers and learners from using it, though they may learn to use it better, as many have.

So, while it is wishful thinking to believe we can stop the tsunami in its tracks, prudence requires that we heed the signals that warn us of the dangers we face, and to recognize that these will only grow in scope. At the same time, we should not assume that AGI has or will develop the capacity to provide *all* the answers to our questions even if it can clarify an enormous number and answer them with considerable speed. AGI maybe be brilliant, but it is not infallible. Some of life's most perplexing questions, says Junaid Mubeen, a distinguished mathematician, simply "do not lend themselves to answers that computers can make meaningful."[15] What we need to do is to understand AGI, learn to manage its use for good, mitigate its negative effects, develop strategies for best practice, and benefit from its potential for serving the world through education, health care, agriculture, and other initiatives for the common good.

My focus in this chapter is, however, not primarily on the use we make of AGI, but on the recognition that AGI is "pregnant with theological significance," and it is so because it raises questions that are fundamental to Christian faith and human well-being, which need to be considered in responding to its challenge.[16] But I

13. Butler, "Black Theology and Artificial Intelligence," 187–92.
14. Singler, "Anthropology and Sociology," 228.
15. Mubeen, *Mathematical Intelligence*, 200.
16. See Dorobantu, "Artificial Intelligence and Christianity," 88.

must confess that when I wrote *Being Human* in 2006,[17] long after Alan Turing coined the term "artificial intelligence" and *Star Wars* introduced me to robots (R2-D2), I made no reference to AI or its implications for being human. In fact, I was blissfully unaware of the discussion about AI that had already been going on for at least a quarter of a century among a handful of theologians who were aware. An example from the 1990s is the discussion around Cog, a robot constructed at MIT, and especially its implications for our understanding of the *imago dei* as relational rather than substantialist.[18]

Despite that lack, I was influenced by the work of theologians of my own and previous generations who were responding to the challenges which modern science presents to Christian faith.[19] Thus while the rise of AI may not have gained my attention, I have long been familiar with some significant theological resources on which we can now draw in responding to its challenge, in addition to those that are now being developed specifically with AGI in mind. Indeed, some of its challenges were already anticipated when Christian theologians first faced the challenges of Hellenistic philosophy as they struggled to define their faith at the birth of Christendom.[20] And in so far as AGI now penetrates virtually every corner of personal and social life, there are connections between its challenge and Bonhoeffer's legacy at several points, not least between the pervasiveness of AI and what he said about restoring "aesthetic existence" in the life of the church as a "sphere of freedom." But let me begin my response by asking Microsoft Copilot for some help in finding the vital or life-giving balance between AIG as a servant of our common good and its menace as the enemy of humanity.

---

17. De Gruchy, *Being Human.*
18. See Foerst, "Cog, a Humanoid Robot."
19. See de Gruchy, "Wisdom & the Threat of Scientism."
20. See Torrance, *Theological Science.*

FINDING THE VITAL BALANCE

"How should we defend, sustain, and enhance our humanity in response to the challenge of AGI?" I asked. "That's the kind of question that hits straight at the soul," Microsoft Copilot replied, because "retaining our humanity means leaning harder into the qualities that make us beautifully unpredictable, emotionally rich, and deeply connected." For that reason, we must "stay curious and reflective, prioritize empathy and relationships, embrace creativity and art, slow down and disconnect, and participate in ethical dialogue." This being so, Copilot recommended that we "resist the pressure to optimize everything . . . go analog—write by hand, take long walks, stare at the stars. Let silence be sacred again." After all, being human "is an act of rebellion against becoming mere data points." Further, Copilot told me, "The world is coded, not us, so it is up to us to decide what part of humanity we most want to hold on to."[21]

In short, Microsoft Copilot was advising me to become a cybertechnic dissenter by taking steps to ensure that the left hemisphere of my brain, the rational and technical, remains grounded in the uniquely human creative and intuitive right hemisphere and so prevents me from being overwhelmed by the analytical, left hemisphere.[22] Seeking to establish this critical balance between the right- and left-hand sides of our brains is more complex than it sounds, for AGI displays an *artificial* creativity that rivals if not exceeds our own, and there is even some discussion about computers as "spiritual machines" who do this.[23] But maintaining a balance between our right and left brain also correlates well with what Bonhoeffer said about recovering "aesthetic existence" in the life of the church in order to keep the left-hand side of our brains under control and prevent ourselves from becoming robots.

---

21. Text generated by Microsoft Copilot, Wednesday July 16, 2025.

22. McGilchrist, *Master and His Emissary*, 191; see also Vernon, *Awake!*, 165. On the relationship between science, especially mathematics, and creativity, see du Sautoy, *Blueprints*.

23. Kurzweil, *Age of Spiritual Machines*.

This possibility is not as bizarre as it may sound. After all, AGI has composed music in the style of Beethoven and the blues that has been played by robotic musicians, and there are reports of a Japanese hotel that is staffed not only by robots who serve tables, but also by robotic chefs who can digest menus from across the globe to create culinary delights. This is impressive, but is it truly intuitive, right-hand brain stuff, or is it technology pushed counterintuitively to the limit, thereby undermining human creativity even while satisfying our appetites and telling us to be creative? AI can undoubtedly write poetry given the necessary algorithms to do so, but it would not be poetry that arises out of the soul.

A few rhetorical questions will illustrate the problem of replacing humans with robots. What if medical science *only* trained highly efficient robotic medics, making human doctors redundant in the same way that technicians and mechanics have become in automobile factories?[24] What if robotic psychologists, who can already diagnose and process clinical information faster and better than humans, *replaced* all human therapists? What if robotic professors *replaced* humans in the lecture hall or in supervising dissertations? Or what if robotic priests heard confessions, pronounced forgiveness, and provided artificial guidance? What if missionary robots spread the "good news" in every language and at great speed, making born-again cyborgs who could quote scripture ad nauseum without any existential engagement? Indeed, what if God became incarnate as a robot instead of becoming fully human and suffering on a cross? Certainly, the Christian understanding of salvation would be totally undermined. As Gregory of Nazianzus, the fourth-century Cappadocian father put it, what God "has not assumed cannot be saved," especially if by salvation we mean, with Saint Irenaeus, the restoration of our humanity![25] As Bonhoeffer observed well before the advent of AI, in seeking to save the world

---

24. See Kohn et al., eds., *To Err Is Human*.

25. Gregory the Theologian, "Letter 101 to Cledonius."; see de Gruchy, *Being Human*, 157–63.

technology often "ruins what it would secure: the human being as human."[26]

Several years after the death of our son Steve, I wrote *Led into Mystery* to deal with my grief and explore the mystery of life and death.[27] The journey began beside a treacherous river in flood where Steve had drowned and still lay trapped beneath the rocks. As Isobel was fetching our daughter from the airport, I was accompanied to the site by a friend of Steve's and of our family, who sat nearby as I shed tears. She offered few words of solace, but in the silence of those dreadful hours her prayerful presence was more comforting than a thousand words uttered by any robot could ever be. And when, ten years later, she died from cancer, grateful for the medical technology that had eased her pain and prolonged her life, she accepted the frailty of our shared humanity, and those who knew her gave thanks for a beautiful human life well lived. Such is both the wonder and the mystery of being human, which robots will never share, and why, despite all our tears and fears, we choose to be human rather than transhuman cyborgs.

In conversing with Bonhoeffer, I have access to all his writings online, but so do robots, who can recall far more accurately and speedily than I the details of his life but have no *sense* of his *lived experience*. So, robots may be useful conversation partners who provide me with information and comment, and even offer words of encouragement, but all these offerings are artificial—the result of conversing with an "it" rather than a "Thou," to use Martin Buber's terminology.[28] Robots are born in a factory not a womb; they are programmed not educated. They are not responsible for what they say, nor do they feel guilty if they advise me badly. They do not live by faith, or in fear and trembling, nor do they fall in love. And they lack *empathy* for those who suffer even if the sufferers happen to be their programmers. So, if they eventually do replace, dehumanize, or annihilate us; they have no awareness of doing so, or regret if it happens. And if they happened to be

26. Bonhoeffer, *Ethics*, 177fn20. See de Gruchy, *Faith Facing Reality*, 79–85.
27. De Gruchy, *Led into Mystery*.
28. See Buber, *I and Thou*, 115.

standing on holy ground, they would never experience awe or express themselves in worship and prayer.

STANDING ON HOLY GROUND

In the end, the perfect self-generating and omnicompetent robot that we strive to produce mirrors the way Ludwig Feuerbach described God—as the projection of our desire for an alter ego that is all-knowing and all-powerful.[29] That is, a god who meets all our perceived needs if we are willing to surrender our humanity, which is, of course, the aim of tyranny and the result of idolatry. The advisors of dictators are mostly yes-men who are programmed to say what their bosses want to hear. In the same way, we humans think of God as an omnipotent Robot or deus ex machina, which, says Bonhoeffer, has been made by us "to solve insoluble problems or to provide strength when human powers fail."[30] The danger is that this can result in the exploitation of our human weaknesses and limitations, so that we lose control and even become subject to what Saint Paul referred to as destructive "principalities and powers."[31] Such a robotic god is not the God who is revealed in Jesus Christ, the God whose saving "power is known through weakness" and whose wisdom seems "foolish" when compared to artificial intelligence, which may often be false rather than always trustworthy.[32] Robotology, then, is no substitute for *lived* theology, that is, the human journey into the mystery beyond our control, whom we name God.[33]

Stephen Fry concludes his account of Homer's *Odyssey* on a sobering note. With this "Promethean myth," he writes, "the Greeks prefigured exactly our AI fears. Zeus wouldn't let these new entities, 'humans,' possess fire—fire the technological transformer,

---

29. Feuerbach, *Essence of Christianity*.

30. Bonhoeffer, *Letters and Papers*, 366.

31. Eph 6:12. See Paul Kingsnorth's radical critique of modernity and technology in *Against the Machine*.

32. 1 Cor 1:18–21.

33. See Olson, *Supremacy*, 53.

the toaster and roaster, melter and smelter, but also fire the *spirit*, the divine spark." So, says Fry, "if a Prometheus[34] amongst us were to give AI consciousness, the divine spark, then humanity could become a mythic memory, an origin story for machines to tell themselves."[35] If Atlantis was submerged by a tidal wave, Prometheus burned himself to death in a raging fire. But the story of Moses being halted in his tracks by a "burning bush that was not consumed" is something very different, and it launches an alternative narrative that has the liberation of slaves from bondage as its goal.[36]

Commanded to shed his sandals because he was "standing on holy ground," Moses is forbidden to transgress the boundary separating humans from God lest he be consumed by fire. Instead, he "hid his face, for he was afraid to *look* at God."[37] Such caution is always a necessary prelude to the journey into the mystery of the God who is beyond human imitation, imagination, and manipulation. God is not a golden calf or mammoth robot we mistakenly think we can control, but a hidden mystery who is revealed as love and justice within the life of the world, and ultimately in the life of God in Jesus Christ, the One who becomes truly human. Moreover, the radical transformation of consciousness or *metanoia* that follows Moses's encounter with God cannot be produced by any "learning machine." On the contrary, it took the liberated slaves forty years of wandering in the wilderness to learn not to trust idols, for if they did, they would return to slavery. The sad truth is that we do not often learn from our mistakes; the present war "to end all wars" is an adage that no longer has credibility. Progress is neither inevitable, nor is it always inevitably good.

In *Technics and Civilization*, published between the First and Second World Wars, Lewis Mumford describes how technological progress has developed most rapidly during times of uncertainty

---

34. Prometheus was a Titan who put power into human hands.
35. Fry, *Odyssey*, 354.
36. Exod 3:1–12.
37. Exod 3:5.

and war, but it inevitably transgresses moral boundaries to do so.[38] Building bigger and better weapons is the prime example, but so is uncontrolled mining and industrial development without care for the welfare of labor or the environment. The material and moral consequences of progress are often recognized by the scientists who pioneer the way, but the power to develop new technologies in the name of progress does not reside with them but with those who finance them, whether governments or business enterprises. This inevitably entrenches power and increases enrichment even if the outcomes also serve the common good.

In sum, then, the "dynamic of civilized existence," as Terry Eagleton describes such hubris, or the Faustian desire for transcendence or supremacy, hollows out our humanity. It creates a spiritual vacuum that we seek to fill "beyond the given to whatever eludes our grasp."[39] With Friedrich Nietzsche we advocate "the transvaluation of values" embodied in *Supermenschen*.[40] Instead of valuing love, humility, and serving the oppressed and the poor, we exalt vitality, strength, and power—the values prized by those who want to develop and use AGI to amass personal wealth and to exert power and influence: hence the development of transhumans, that is people with superior intelligence and strength as a result of genetic engineering and cybernetic implants—human-robot hybrids.

To appreciate the danger of this development we need to briefly trace the development of transhumanism from its origins in the eugenics movement in England that was led by the evolutionary biologist Julian Huxley in the 1940s but then took on a sinister significance in Nazi Germany's program to purify the nation. Huxley coined the term "transhuman" to distance his project from Nazi eugenics, which sought to give scientific respectability to sterilizing and murdering genetically "inferior" people. For Huxley, transhumanism was about using science to guide evolution to improve society, not to cull those deemed inferior subhumans. But

---

38. Mumford, *Technics and Civilization*, 163–72, 182–85.
39. Eagleton, *Culture*, 26.
40. Nietzsche, *Will to Power*.

the attempt by AGI to enhance the human mind "by merging it with intelligent machines"[41] to produce a more intelligent human species is treading on dangerous ground that can easily lead to genocide.

The fact that we are not currently doing well at embodying and pursuing values that encourage taking care of creation, overcoming poverty, caring for the disabled, or preventing war, increases the temptation to capitulate to robots and their agents, who can do the job for us. But the solution does not lie in outsourcing our human responsibility and developing more sophisticated technologies. It requires a transformation of consciousness and a proactive defense of humanity and of the earth, humanity's home. The unsettling truth is that we cannot assume that everyone is considered truly human either by ourselves or by others, especially those regarded as enemies. Nor can we assume that we always know what it means to be human and live accordingly.

CHOOSING TO BE HUMAN

Not so long ago, when I went online to do my banking, I was asked for my name and code. These days I am asked whether I am a human. But my bank does not really want to know about my grief and sorrow, nor whether I care about life or love another human; it is not interested in my humanity at all: it just wants to be assured that I am not a robot and therefore can be held responsible for my online activities. Having for so long been defined by genealogy, ethnicity, gender, class and religion, I find that the question comes as a refreshing surprise. Irrespective of the reason, some robot wants to know that I am human! Indeed, the cybertechnological revolution depends on this, as does online advertising, surveillance, and the use of AI programs themselves.

My immediate response is to check the box and do my banking. But I pause to reflect on the significance of the question because it makes me think about what it means to be human. And

---

41. See Olson, *Supremacy*, 74.

part of being human is that I must affirm what I am—neither Microsoft Copilot nor Perplexity can do that for me. They can provide an accurate and comprehensive outline of the story of my life culled from various sources in their own data banks. But they cannot tell my story even if they normally get the details correct, for there is no way they can know who I really am. Even Isobel, my soulmate for more than sixty years, who knows me better than anyone, will confess that she doesn't fully know me, nor do I always know myself if the truth be told. Discovering who we are is part of our journey into the mystery we name God, for in the end, as Bonhoeffer reminds us in trying to understand himself, God alone knows.[42] That is of no interest to the bank or to Amazon.com.

But what if during the apartheid years I had been asked not whether I was white or Black, but human? What if during those years the South African regime had not asked me to identify my ethnicity when applying for a job, a house, or a place in school, but had asked simply whether I was human and, by implication, whether I had the same needs and aspirations, fears, doubts and hopes as every other human even if we were of different ethnicities? That might not have prevented racism, but it would have alerted me to the fact that apartheid was a crime against humanity. To be asked whether I am human forces me, then, to ask who I really am *as a human being*, and whether my neighbor or enemy is an "it" at my disposal or human like me. Once again, there is no way that AGI can answer such existential questions for me any more than I can for others. In any case, neither my bank nor any other online business is really interested to know about my relationships with other humans because the system does not understand that I cannot be human on my own.

To be human, as Bishop Desmond Tutu taught us in the struggle for justice and reconciliation, is always expressed in relationship with others; we cannot be persons in isolation.[43] "An injury to one is an injury to all," was our chanted conviction. This

---

42. Bonhoeffer, *Letters and Papers*, 460.
43. Based on the isiXhosa saying: "ubuntu ungamntu ngabanye abantu." See Battle, *Reconciliation*, 39.

is not a denial of our unique personalities, but a recognition that we cannot truly live and flourish in isolation from other humans. Robots do not get lonely; humans do. As Tutu cautioned, "a self-sufficient human being is subhuman."[44] That is why keeping prisoners in isolation is inhumane or soul destroying. If we capitulate to the control of AGI, we will not become Nietzsche's transhuman *Supermenschen* but *Untermenschen*—dehumanized serfs waiting to be declared redundant, dismantled, or incinerated. Choosing to be human is a protest against being dehumanized.

Checking the box and choosing to be human also means that I am an agent who is responsible for my actions, and by extension, not just those actions that relate to my bank account, but also those that relate to other humans and to our shared habitat. This implies that I must join with others in ensuring that robots, if they are to be useful, must serve the common good rather than serve the greed and "will-to-power" of those who want to be *Supermenschen*. Being human also implies that I can and should acknowledge my failures and change my ways if required. Robots cannot do that either for me or for themselves, even if they acknowledge errors and say sorry with a simulated accent. To belabor the point, this is a critical difference between humans and androids: AGI machines, no matter how sophisticated, are not morally responsible agents, and such agency lies at the heart of the problem facing us.

Apartheid was labeled a "crime against humanity," and the attempt to justify it as Christian was declared a heresy. But the criminals and heretics were the people who advocated and supported the policies, not the policies themselves, wrong as they were. Crimes against humanity are always perpetrated by humans, irrespective of their instruments. Humans are guilty, not technology; drones cannot be taken to the International Court of Justice, tyrants can. But when robots begin to act on their own volition and even achieve "digital immortality," they are beyond the control

---

44. This line was from "God's Dream," a speech Tutu gave at the Nuclear Age Peace Foundation's annual dinner on May 10, 1990. The speech was published in Krieger and Kelly, eds., *Waging Peace II*, and is cited here quoted in Battle, *Reconciliation*, 35.

of even their creators.[45] No wonder their creators are alarmed. This was already sensed by the mad scientist played by Peter Sellars in the 1964 movie *Dr. Strangelove*. Instead of banning the bomb they created out of fear, the nuclear-armored nations of the world "fell in love" with "the bomb" as the guarantee of peace. How bizarre is that!

To be asked by a robot whether I am human is, of course, not just an anthropological question, but a profoundly *theological* exercise which opens up a conversation that has far-reaching personal, ecclesial, pastoral, political, and ecological consequences. It has to do with who we are, and how we live and relate to each other and the world. It has to do with the well-being of the planet and future generations. Indeed, it forces us to consider whether there is an ultimate source of value that determines whether being human is important, and if so, who or what this source may be—that is, who *for us* is God and who are we *for God*. That is, it requires us to decide what constitutes the essence of our humanity, and whether we desire to gain the whole world even if we lose our souls in the process and become heartless robots.

SALVAGING OUR SOULS

Early in 1944 Bonhoeffer sent a homily from prison to his godson, Dietrich Bethge, on the occasion of his baptism. He wrote: "If we come through the wreckage of a lifetime's acquired goods with our living souls (*lebendige Seele*) intact, let us be satisfied with that." He went on to say: "It will be the task of our generation, not to 'seek great things,' but to save and preserve our souls out of the chaos." For the soul will empower us "to plan and build up and give shape to a new and better life."[46] Bonhoeffer was not writing about saving some ghostlike mannikin from the world for some future disembodied heaven, but of salvaging our humanity, our *Seele* or "souls" in order to rebuild the world.

---

45. Delio, "Transhumanism and Transcendence," 144–45.
46. Bonhoeffer, *Letters and Papers*, 387.

Several key words relating to being human are used in the New Testament. I will provide the original Hellenistic Greek alongside the English equivalents in discussing their meanings.[47] The words are ψυχή (*psyche*, or *anima* in Latin): normally translated as "soul," it refers to a person's "interior life," his or her emotions, desires, and will; πνεύμά (*pneuma*) is "spirit" or "breath," often used in relation to "life"; and νους (mind), refers to our "consciousness" and the ability to reason. By contrast, σάρχ (*sarx*) or "flesh" refers to the physical body or to sinful human nature depending on context, and σώμά (*soma*) refers to the "body," that is, the physical structure of a human being or animal. If ψυχή (*psyche*) infused with πνεύμά (spirit) and νους (mind) describes us humans being "alive" (that is, *lebendig*, in Bonhoeffer's parlance), then taken together with σάρχ (flesh) and σώμά (body), the combination in total refers to humans as "embodied souls": that is, these words convey a holistic understanding of being human. As the medieval mystic Julian of Norwich said, the soul has to do with "the very fact that *we exist.*"[48] Not as inanimate machines but as living, breathing or animated souls, or in Bonhoeffer's language, *lebendige Seele*.

Whatever the literal meaning of these words, the way in which we understand and use them today opens up a proverbial can of worms. Not only do "body," "mind," "self," "person," and "consciousness" have a history in English discourse such that their meanings have been hotly debated and divided philosophers and theologians, but loosely defined, they are also part of our daily conversation and religious rhetoric. The fact that these words also translate words used in other religious traditions (e.g. Buddhism), and that there is also a debate about their meaning within those traditions, makes clarity even more confusing at times. But it is noteworthy that the word "soul," unlike the other words, disappeared from philosophical discourse, though not from popular discourse, in the West following the eighteenth-century Enlightenment. This

---

47. See the following articles in *TDNT*: Kleinknecht, "πνεύμά"; Schweizer, "σάρχ"; Schweizer, "σώμά"; Dihle, "ψυχή." Compare the discussion of John 1:14 in Brown, *John*, 31–32; and Barrett, *John*, 164–65.

48. See Rolf, *Julian's Gospel*, 495.

was largely under the influence of René Descartes's body-mind dualism, which he summed up as "I think therefore I am" (*cognito, ergo sum*)—that is, the fact that I think proves that I exist. By the twentieth century, many in secular society were convinced with Gilbert Ryle even if they had never heard of him, that while we have minds that consciously think, there is no "ghost in the machine."[49] That is, humans are not mindless, but we are soulless.

Descartes's dualism was foreshadowed in much ancient Greek philosophy, which distinguished the *psyche*, understood as the immortal self, from the physical, mortal body, or *soma*.[50] This found radical expression in Manichaeism, a gnostic cult that thrived in early Christendom even claiming Saint Augustine's allegiance before his conversion to Christianity. But under different names it keeps on sneaking back into popular religious understanding, especially in bad times.[51] For the Manichees, the body, or *sarx*, is "fallen" nature, and the material world (including the body) is evil. By contrast, the soul, or *psyche*, is a fragment of the divine essence held captive in the body. Salvation, from this perspective, implies the release of the soul from its fleshly captivity through interior illumination and initiation into the cult.[52]

Gnosticism was rejected by the early church chiefly for its downgrading of the physical body as evil. Nothing was a more decisive counter to this than the prologue to the Fourth Gospel (the "Word became flesh [*sarx*] and lived among us"),[53] the Nicene Creed's affirmation of Jesus Christ as both "truly God and truly human," and belief in the "resurrection of the body" as distinct from belief in an independent "immortal soul."[54] Indeed, as Saint

---

49. Ryle, *Concept of Mind*.

50. See Cornford, Introduction, xxv; Brown, "Soul," 676–85.

51. Augustine, *Confessions* 3.5-8 (in Augustine, *"Confessions" and "Enchiridion,"* ed. Outler, 66–75).

52. See Kelly, *Early Christian Doctrines*, 8–9.

53. John 1:14.

54. See Irenaeus on "Flesh, Soul, and Spirit," *Adversus Haeresis* 5.9.1, in Bettenson, ed. and trans., *Early Christian Fathers*, 70–71; Cullmann, *Immortality of the Soul or Resurrection of the Dead?*

Augustine came to insist, we can only know reality "through the senses of the body," for the invisible is understood from what we experience bodily, that is, from the visible.[55] This was not only a categorical rejection of the gnostic disparagement of the body, but as Harnack, Bonhoeffer's teacher, argued, also a declaration that God's justice "would triumph over evil, giving us an eternal hope, and fulfilling the desires of the oppressed."[56] It is in this sense that Christians speak metaphorically of the "immortality of the soul" as a mystery which, said the Second Vatican Council "utterly beggars the imagination."[57]

Despite this clarification, not only did "soul language" depart both from the vocabulary and the consciousness of a largely secular, educated Western world, but modern theologians, such as Reinhold Niebuhr in *The Self and the Dramas of History*, substituted "self" for "soul" in translating *psyche*. This not only distinguished the word "self" from notions of reincarnation, but it was the preferred term in social psychology.[58] Theologically "soul" was now understood as "human nature in its self-awareness."[59] But clearly the Christian understanding of "self" is different from secular variations. As Niebuhr himself acknowledged, it "distinguishes itself by a yearning for the ultimate" or transcendence.[60] "Self" is simply inadequate for expressing the longing of a "soul" thirsting "for the living God."[61] This is also acknowledged by Rowan Williams when, in *The Passions of the Soul* (a phrase used earlier by Descartes to

---

55. St. Augustine, *Confessions* 10.6 (see Augustine, *"Confessions" and "Enchiridion,"* ed. Outler, 206n16).

56. See Kelly, *Early Christian Creeds*, 163–65; Harnack, *Mission and Expansion of Christianity*, 92.

57. See Abbott, ed., *Documents of Vatican II*, 215. See also Ratzinger, "Dignity of the Human Person"; and Ratzinger, "Reality of Life After Death."

58. Niebuhr, *Self and the Dramas of History*; see also Mead, *Mind, Self & Society*.

59. Klinger, "Soul," 1615.

60. Niebuhr, *Self and the Dramas of History*, 5; see also de Gruchy, *Led into Mystery*, 211–14.

61. Ps 42:1–2.

describe nothing more than "emotional intelligence"), he speaks of the "interiority" not just of the "self" but of the "authentic self."[62]

The problem is, as Werner Heisenberg, a prominent German nuclear physicist (who worked closely with Bonhoeffer's brother Karl Friedrich at the University of Leipzig in the 1930s) said, we do not keep in touch with reality through science, but "through tried and tested human intuitions about consciousness, the soul or God which 'touch reality' in a way that scientific concepts do not."[63] Undoubtedly this is one reason why "soul language" has made a major comeback today. And not too soon, for some now claim that AGI is on the verge of creating self-conscious robots.[64]

Already in 2000, in an article on the "soul" in *The Oxford Companion to Christian Thought*, Peter Hebblethwaite speculated that if AI becomes "the vehicle of inner life" (subjectivity, reason, and will), then its "artefacts" (i.e. robots) "would have acquired selfhood, soul and spirit, and would have to be treated and related to in just the same way as are our children."[65] We would then find ourselves having to learn how to use not only a machine with a mind of its own, but one that could claim the right to be treated as human. The legal implications of that, to say nothing else, are mind-boggling. Imagine a robot taking us to court on charges of discrimination because we decided to employ a human instead. Though I think it is more likely that humans will be treated as machines and human rights law will be impotent to protect us. Bonhoeffer was remarkably prescient, then, when in Nazi Germany he warned that technology would become "an end in itself" with its "own soul" (*eigene Seele*). He also said that even if a "naïve faith" protests this development, the process cannot be reversed.[66] But being self-conscious is not what make us who we are as humans. If

---

62. Williams, *Passions of the Soul*; see also Williams, *On Christian Theology*, 239–50.

63. See Heisenberg, *Physics & Philosophy*, 188, as quoted in Vernon, *Awake!*, 74.

64. See also de Gruchy, "Retrieving the Soul."

65. Hebblethwaite, "Soul."

66. Bonhoeffer, *Ethics*, 116.

we lose consciousness as a result of an accident, we don't cease to be "living souls" (*lebendige Seele*). What distinguishes us humans from robots is not only that we have bodies of flesh and blood, rather than being plastic conglomerates, but that we are "embodied souls"—that is, we have a sense of the transcendent. And that, theologically speaking, is because *human* beings are created in the "image of God."[67] For Christians, if not for secularists, this clearly has far-reaching consequences for the way we understand ourselves and relate to each other as well as to the world.

So how can we bring "soul language," the language of the "embodied" or "living soul," back into contemporary discourse and retrieve its potency in response to the reductionism of AGI? Maybe some analogies, imperfect as they are, will provide helpful clues. For example, furniture maker George Nakashima uses "soul language" to describe that which lies beneath the bark of a tree but makes it attractive to the eye and is "resurrected" in furniture that gives new form to its beauty. This corresponds with Saint Thomas's definition of the soul as the "form of the body," that is, that which gives it an identity and purpose.[68] Mahalia Jackson used "soul language" to express the "feelings" evoked by African American spirituals, such as those that transformed Bonhoeffer's life.[69] And Jim Wallis speaks of the "soul of politics" when referring to the universal moral values that shape public policy for the common good.[70]

"Soul" is, then, the language both of passion and feeling, and of moral value and dignity. With regard to the first, it is an affirmation, with Wolfgang Huber, that we "humans belong not only to the species *Homo sapiens* but also to the species '*homo sentiens*.'"[71]

---

67. See LaCugna, *God for Us*, 93–96; Dorobantu, "Artificial Intelligence and Christianity," 92–95.

68. See Nakashima, *Soul of a Tree*; Thomas Aquinas, *Summa Theologiae*, 108–9.

69. Floyd, *Power of Black Music*, 203; Young, *No Difference in the Fare*, 168–69.

70. Wallis, *Soul of Politics*, xvi–xvii.

71. Huber, "What Does It Mean to Tell the Truth?," 35.

Modern medical technology replaced a valve in my heart so that it could better function as a pump, for which I am exceedingly grateful. But I am more than a machine, which is why only "soul language" could mend my "broken heart" when our son Steve tragically died. The truth is, we are empathetic organisms who cannot live on secondhand information when we need wisdom and empathy. Which is why, cautions Harari, we cannot "trust computer algorithms to make wise decisions and create a better world."[72] Only the "authentic self," that is, the "soul," can be a moral agent.

This brings us to the second dimension of "soul language"—it is the language of moral value and dignity. Whatever else robots might be or become, they do not have the ability to value life and respect human dignity.[73] That is, they do not recognize what Harnack described as the "infinite value of the soul," something fundamentally different from the utilitarian value of robots.[74] Such value is based not on merit, or human usefulness (like forced labor), but on being human in the "image of God."[75] It is this inherent quality, not human need or capacity, that provides the Christian basis for the recognition of human dignity.[76] Thus in describing humans as "embodied souls," the Second Vatican Council reaffirmed the dignity of being human in all its complexity: the mind and body as well as truth, wisdom, conscience, and responsible freedom, which even death cannot expunge or defeat.[77] No robot can match such dignity, nor is there any reason why it should, for the value of robots and humans lies in their difference, not their sameness, irrespective of their likeness. Humans can love even though they are not perfect; robots can be machined to perfection, but they cannot love.

72. Harari, *Nexus*, xxiii.
73. Pope Francis, *Hope*, 281.
74. Harnack, *What Is Christianity?*, 63; see Bonhoeffer, *Discipleship*, 84n1.
75. See Forrester, *On Human Worth*, 83–84.
76. See Moltmann, *On Human Dignity*; Wolterstorff, *Journey Toward Justice*, 48–49.
77. See Abbott, ed., *Documents of Vatican II*, 210–14.

NONCONFORMING COMMUNITIES

In concluding *Nexus*, a critical assessment of AGI, Harari writes: we "need to build institutions that will be able to check not just familiar human weaknesses like greed and hatred, but also radically alien errors" that destroy our humanity and the planet.[78] The ecumenical or global church (understood in all its complexity) is one such institution, but unlike most others, its primary reason for existence is to "salvage souls." The church cannot do what governments or universities must do to regulate AGI, but it must surely do what Barth insists it do in *Against the Stream*: that is, "be the church."[79]

With this in mind, I suggest that the time has come to establish and foster intentional communities within the life of the church, communities whose specific calling and task is to develop a nonconforming lifestyle and dissenting strategy that that enables the church to use AGI for the common good while at the same time resisting its dehumanizing power. In doing so the church would once again become a "sphere of freedom," not only by being an inclusive community of prayer and working for justice, but by enabling us to affirm our humanity and salvage our souls.

Therefore the mission of the church in a world dominated by AGI is nothing less than embodying and defending the integrity of humanity—a task that is implicit in the Nicene Creed when we confess that God became fully human in Jesus Christ for the sake of humanity (not just religious folk) fulfilled and restored to life in Christ.[80] This was fundamental to Bonhoeffer's ecclesiology from the time he wrote *Sanctorum Communio* until he began to envisage the "church for others" in prison. The church, for him, was nothing less than the "vicarious representation" of Christ in the world. That is, "God's new will and purpose for humanity."[81] He is not thinking here of the church primarily as an institution but, as he later

---

78. Hariri, *Nexus*, 301.
79. Barth, "Christian Message and the New Humanism," 190–92.
80. Rom 5:1–20.
81. Bonhoeffer, *Sanctorum Communio*, 141.

describes it, as a community of people in "whom Christ is taking form."[82] Indeed, in Christ a new humanity already exists, which by its very existence challenges every attempt to create a transhuman "superhumanity" (*Übermenschentum*) that attempts "to outgrow [our] nature as human."[83] In this way the church confronts the dehumanizing power of hubris even before it utters a word. As Bonhoeffer says, we should "not underestimate the significance of the human 'example'" that "has its origin in the humanity of Jesus."[84]

In refusing to be seduced by the temptation to grasp power and triumphally conform to Christendom or Empire, the church shares in what Saint Paul calls God's ministry of restraint.[85] That is, restraining those forces that are preventing the coming of God's reign of equity, justice, and peace. Or, as Hariri puts it, such restraint helps keep in check the "familiar human weaknesses like greed and hatred" and "radically alien errors,"[86] among them spreading falsehoods. In being the church, the church should be at the forefront of combatting "fake news" and telling the truth, a subject that preoccupied Bonhoeffer prior to his arrest.[87]

Telling the truth was, in fact, a critical issue within the Resistance itself and, as Huber points out, what Bonhoeffer learned about the relationship between truth, relationships, and the complex realities of that time has contemporary relevance for the life and witness of the church in our digital age. "Truth," says Huber, summarizing Bonhoeffer's argument, "represents the openness of our world and our existence before God." Therefore, truth is "embedded in reality." To tell the truth means unmasking conflicts "in order to open the way to reconciliation" in the struggle for

---

82. Bonhoeffer, *Ethics*, 97

83. Bonhoeffer, *Ethics*, 94; see de Gruchy, *Being Human*, 163–72.

84. Bonhoeffer, *Letters and Papers*, 503–4.

85. See 2 Thess 2:6–7. See Wanamaker, *Epistles to the Thessalonians*, 252–53.

86. Hariri, *Nexus*, 301.

87. See Bonhoeffer, "What Does It Mean to Tell the Truth?"; see also Bonhoeffer, *Letters and Papers*, 223.

justice and peace.[88] This takes us to the crux of the matter, because right now the danger of AGI being manipulated and getting out of control is through its spreading hatred and promoting violence and war. For this reason, the transformation of consciousness in contrast to Nietzsche's "transformation of values" is central to the pastoral task of the church in restraining the powers of AGI.

The need for the "transformation of consciousness" relates then, to what Bonhoeffer meant by the recovery of "aesthetic existence" in the life of the church as a "sphere of freedom," or what the poet-theologian William Blake called a "perceptual openness" that enables us to see reality from a transcendent perspective without bias or illusion.[89] If Blake's dissenting views were somewhat heterodox, I suggest that Rowan Williams discerns a similar connection between "liberated action and perception" in the eighteenth-century Greek Orthodox *Philokalia*, which provides a "powerful critical perspective on the mechanisms of acquisitiveness, the myths of human autonomy and isolation from the material universe and the techniques of silencing or dehumanizing what challenges these myths and mechanisms."[90]

Clearly this is not a pious way of escape from political engagement or from responding positively to genuine technological progress, but rather a prophetic imagining of redemptive possibilities in the struggle for a more humane world. And that is what Bonhoeffer meant when he said in "After Ten Years" that he now saw "happiness and misfortune, strength and weakness with new eyes" and thus had a clearer understanding of "greatness, humanness, justice, and mercy." In addition, he had come to see "that personal suffering is a more useful key ... than personal happiness for exploring the meaning of the world in contemplation and action."[91]

So, in conclusion, I return to where I began in reflecting on Christian dissent, which is nowhere better expressed than by Saint Paul's in his Letter to the Romans. Having provided a majestic

---

88. Huber, "What Does It Mean to Tell the Truth?," 32, 38.
89. Blake, "Marriage of Heaven and Hell," 154; see Vernon, *Awake!*, 2, 39.
90. Williams, *Passions of the Soul*, xii–xiii.
91. Bonhoeffer, *Letters and Papers*, 52.

overview of the gospel (chapters 1–11), he tells the church, a small and harassed community at the heart of the empire, not to conform "to this present age" but rather to be "transformed by the renewing of the mind (νοος)" by offering their "bodies" (σώματα) to the service of God and allowing their "minds" or "consciousness" (νοος) to be transformed. Only by doing this will they be able to "discern the will of God" and do what is "good and perfect."[92]

---

92. Rom 12:1–2 (my translation).

Epilogue
A Sense of Time Fulfilled

> Time is the most precious gift at our disposal, being of all gifts the most irretrievable, the thought of time possibly lost disturbs us whenever we look back. Time is lost when we have not lived, experienced things, learned, worked, enjoyed, and suffered as human beings. Lost time is unfulfilled, empty time.
>
> —Bonhoeffer[1]

SOON AFTER HIS IMPRISONMENT in Tegel Military Prison in Berlin, on April 5, 1943, Bonhoeffer began to plan "a small study on the sense of time," which would make his past present" to himself "in a situation in which time could so easily appear 'empty' and 'lost.'"[2] He never executed that plan, but he did jot down some cryptic notes on the subject.[3] These reveal his inner turmoil as he struggled to come to terms with his new situation, his pending trial and his forced separation from his family, friends, and fiancée, Maria. And, lurking in his consciousness was his knowledge of the plot being planned to assassinate Adolf Hitler, of which he was a part.

---

1. Bonhoeffer, *Letters and Papers*, 37.
2. Bonhoeffer, *Letters and Papers*, 71, 98, 106.
3. Bonhoeffer, *Letters and Papers*, 70–74.

Going Against the Stream

Bonhoeffer's jottings on time may lack structure, but they vividly reveal the mental turmoil of those initial weeks in prison as he struggled to avoid "self-deception" and "idealizing the past," as he dealt with "fading memories" and the danger of "self-pity." He speaks of "the ravages and emptiness of time" and "the lack of fulfillment," of time as torment and enemy, as well as friend and healer. He complains of boredom and impatience, speaks of a yearning for freedom and familiar company, and notes the need for a sense of humor in "passing" or "killing" time. Overarching all is his sense of "waiting for death" and being separated "from what is past and what is to come." He refers to being tempted to commit "suicide" because he already feels "practically dead," so that when death finally comes it would be like the closing of a book.[4] But he finds a modicum of consolation from the cynical slogan that a former inmate had scratched above his cell door: "In one hundred years everything will be over."[5] But scattered among these depressing notes and a passing mention of "remorse," there are those that speak of gratitude, and the help he receives from prayer in overcoming his circumstances as he recalls the words of the psalmist: "My times are in your hand, deliver me from the hand of my enemies and persecutors."[6]

Bonhoeffer included some of these thoughts in the poignant letter to his parents on May 15, 1943, in which he also expressed the wish "to at least briefly see or speak" with them to ease his "internal tension." Describing his way of passing the time while anticipating more to come, he tells them:

> I read, reflect, work, write, pace the room—and I really do so without rubbing myself sore on the wall like a polar bear. What matters is being focused on what one still has and what can be done—and that is still a great deal—and on restraining within oneself the rising thoughts about

---

4. See my discussion in de Gruchy, *This Monastic Moment*, 159–60.
5. Bonhoeffer, *Letters and Papers*, 72.
6. Ps 31:15

what one cannot do and the inner restlessness and resentment about the entire situation.[7]

Random as his thoughts now appear, they reflect the shift that circumstances had forced on him: from living an intensely active life in *kairos* time to the numbing life in a prison cell governed by chronological time. But ten months later, in a letter written on March 1, 1944, Bonhoeffer tells Bethge that he is "making a new start at using this last part of my time here as intensively as possible." Indeed, he continues, the "daily threat to life most of us experience at present spurs us like nothing else to fill each moment, to 'make the most of the time.'"[8] "And, sometimes I think I will go on living as long as I have a truly great goal to work for."[9]

Bonhoeffer now structures the time at his disposal by recognizing the passing of the seasons, remembering family birthdays, and celebrating the rhythms of the Christian year. His prison cell takes on the character of a monk's cell, and his understanding of the imposed discipline of prison life resembles the hours of a Benedictine monastery such as he had previously come to appreciate. He practices *lectio divina*, meditates daily on the Moravian *Losungen* and the Psalms, prays and silently sings his favorite hymns. Of course, like Luther and virtually all monastics, he experiences the "noon day demon," acedia, when the "peace and serenity by which one had been carried are suddenly shaken without any apparent physical or psychological reason" and "evil powers . . . seek to rob one of what is most essential."[10] But "even these experiences," he says, "may be good and necessary in order to learn to understand human life better."[11]

Bonhoeffer also read widely, using both the prison library and books he received from his family, many of them referred to

---

7. Bonhoeffer, *Letters and Papers*, 79.
8. A reference to Eph, 5:16; Bonhoeffer, *Letters and Papers*, 311.
9. Bonhoeffer, *Letters and Papers*, 311.
10. Bonhoeffer, *Letters and Papers*, 79; see also de Gruchy, *This Monastic Moment*, 158–60.
11. Bonhoeffer, *Letters and Papers*, 205.

and discussed in his letters.¹² And he spent much time writing. Inter alia, he wrote a "Report on Experiences during Alarms"¹³ and drafted his "Last Will and Testament" (instructing Bethge about the arrangements he had made in case of his death);¹⁴ he crafted a set of "Prayers for Prisoners" at the request of the prison chaplain, Harald Poelchau;¹⁵ and he wrote a wedding sermon for the marriage of Eberhard and Renate Bethge in May 1943, and a year later, a baptismal sermon for their son, Dietrich.¹⁶ But he never wrote his promised essay on a "Sense of Time." Instead, he wrote poetry and started work on a book about "Christianity in a World Come of Age." This launched him into a conversation by underground mail with Eberhard Bethge, beginning with his letter of June 30, 1944, and ending with that of August 23, 1944. Then, on July 20 the plot on Hitler's life failed, and Bonhoeffer instinctively knew that his fate was virtually sealed. Time was fast running out.

Bonhoeffer was martyred on the April 9, 1945, shortly before the war reached its tragic finale. He still had much to look forward to, not least his marriage to Maria. That was not to be, but, as Bethge wrote in his postscript to *Love Letters from Cell 92*, something else did result from the brutally abrupt end to their hopes—nothing less than "a liberated life-affirming theology whose influence has been more profound and far-reaching than anyone would have suspected."¹⁷ I was privileged to meet Maria von Wedemeyer at the Second International Bonhoeffer Congress held in Geneva 1976, and to have some conversation with her afterwards at the Geneva airport. She died aged fifty-three from cancer on November 16, 1977.

---

12. See the list of literature which he mentioned in his correspondence. Bonhoeffer, *Letters and Papers*, 616–25.

13. Bonhoeffer, *Letters and Papers*, 205.

14. Bonhoeffer, *Letters and Papers*, 60, 193–94.

15. Bonhoeffer, *Letters and Papers*, 194–98.

16. Bonhoeffer, *Letters and Papers*, 82–87, 383–90.

17. Bonhoeffer and von Wedemeyer, *Love Letters from Cell 92*, 314, see also Lukens and Bethge, "'By Powers of Good.'"

Epilogue

We visited the Bethges several times in their retirement in Villiprot-Wachtberg near Bonn and invariably went on excursions together.[18] On two occasions we visited Maria Laach the famous Benedictine Monastery which as it happened played an important role in Bonhoeffer's life.[19] The first occasion was in 1993. Eberhard was in his element as we marvelled at the magnificent library and talked to the monks. Later that day, we marvelled again though differently when we visited the Palatine Chapel in Aachen where Charlemagne, one of the last and greatest emperors in the Holy Roman Empire, was buried in 814.

On our second visit to Maria Laach three years later, Eberhard was too frail to wander around, so we sat in the cafeteria and reminisced. He died at the age of ninety on March 18, 2000, the day I turned sixty-one. While Bonhoeffer's life was cut short in its prime, Eberhard, as Wolfgang Huber said at his funeral, not only lived much longer but also lived a fulfilled and well-rounded life.[20] And now in our late eighties, Isobel and I are full of gratitude for a lifelong conversation made possible by the Bethges when, from the early 1970s on, they welcomed us into their home at Rengsdorf and began opening doors that we could hardly have dreamt possible when I first began to explore Bonhoeffer's legacy.

---

18. De Gruchy, *Daring, Trusting Spirit*, 196–202.
19. See, de Gruchy, *This Monastic Moment,* 122.
20. See de Gruchy, *Daring, Trusting Spirit,* 214

Bibliography

Abbot, Walter M., SJ, ed. *The Documents of Vatican II*. Translated by Joseph Gallagher. London: Chapman, 1966.

Aristotle. *The Ethics of Aristotle: The Nichomachean Ethics*. Translated by J. A. K. Thomson. Harmondsworth, UK: Penguin, 1955.

Augustine. *"Confessions" and "Enchiridion."* Edited and translated by Albert C. Outler. LCC 7. London: SCM, 1955.

———. *The Trinity*. Edited by John E. Rotelle. Translated, with introduction and notes, by Edmund Hill, OP. The Works of Saint Augustine, pt. 1, vol. 5. Brooklyn: New City, 1991.

Awasthi, Yogesh, and George Okumu Achar. "African Christian Theology in the Age of AI: Machine Intelligence and Theology in Africa." *Journal of Research in Humanities and Social Science* 13.1 (2025) 207–16.

Bainton, Roland H. *Christian Unity and Religion in New England*. Collected Papers in Church History, ser. 3. London: Hodder & Stoughton, 1965.

Balcomb Anthony, and Phillippe Denis. "Introduction." In "The Contested Legacy of the *Kairos Document.*" Special issue, *Journal of Theology for Southern Africa* 177 (2023) 4–9.

Balthasar, Hans Urs von. *The Glory of the Lord: A Theological Aesthetics*. Vol. 1, *Seeing the Form*. Edinburgh: T. & T. Clark, 1982.

Barr, James, *Biblical Words for Time*. Studies in Biblical Theology 33. London: SCM, 1962.

Barrett, C. K. *A Commentary on the Epistle to the Romans*. Harper's New Testament Commentaries. New York: Harper, 1957.

———. *The Gospel According to St John*. 2nd ed. London: SPCK 1978.

Barth, Karl. "The Christian Message and the New Humanism." In *Against the Stream: Shorter Post-War Writings, 1946–52*, 181–92. Edited and translated by Ronald Gregor Smith. London: SCM, 1954.

———. *Church Dogmatics*. Vol. IV/I, *The Doctrine of Reconciliation, Part 1*. Edited by G. W. Bromiley and T. F. Torrance. Translated by G. W. Bromiley. Edinburgh: T. & T. Clark, 1956 Reprint, 1961.

———. *The Humanity of God*. Translated by John Newton Thomas and Thomas Wieser. Richmond: John Knox, 1960.

BIBLIOGRAPHY

———. *Theological Existence Today!* Translated by R. Birch Hoyle. London: Hodder & Stoughton, 1933.

Battle, Michael. *Reconciliation: The Ubuntu Theology of Desmond Tutu.* Cleveland, OH: Pilgrim, 1997.

Bax, Douglas S. *A Different Gospel: A Critique of the Theology Behind Apartheid.* Johannesburg: Presbyterian Church of Southern Africa, 1979.

Begbie, Jeremy S. *Abundantly More: The Theological Promise of the Arts in a Reductionist World.* Grand Rapids: Baker Academic, 2023.

Bender, Harold S. "The Anabaptist Vision." In *The Recovery of the Anabaptist Vision: A Sixtieth Anniversary Tribute to Harold S. Bender*, edited by Guy F. Hershberger, 29–54. Scottdale, PA: Herald, 1957.

Bethge, Eberhard. "Bonhoeffer's Theology of Friendship." In *Friendship and Resistance: Essays on Dietrich Bonhoeffer*, 86–104. Geneva: WCC Publications, 1995.

———. *Dietrich Bonhoeffer: Theologian, Christian, Man For His Times; A Biography.* Rev. ed. Minneapolis: Fortress, 2000.

Bettenson, Henry Scowcroft, ed. and trans. *The Early Christian Fathers.* London: Oxford University Press, 1956.

Blake, William. "The Marriage of Heaven and Hell." In *The Complete Writings of William Blake: With Variant Readings*, edited by Geoffrey Keynes, 149–62. New ed. Standard Authors Series. London: Oxford University Press, 1966.

Blanke, Fritz. "Anabaptism and the Reformation." In *The Recovery of the Anabaptist Vision*, edited by Guy F. Hershberger, 57–68. Scottdale, PA: Herald, 1957.

Boesak, Allan. *Black and Reformed: Apartheid, Liberation, and the Calvinist Tradition.* Edited by Leonard Sweetman. Maryknoll, NY: Orbis, 1984.

Bonhoeffer, Dietrich. *Act and Being.* Edited by Wayne Whitson Floyd, Jr. Translated by H. Martin Rumscheidt. DBWE 2. Minneapolis: Fortress, 1996.

———. *Barcelona, Berlin, New York, 1928–1931.* Edited by Clifford J. Green. Translated by Douglas W. Stott. DBWE 10. Minneapolis: Fortress, 2008.

———. *Berlin, 1932–1933.* Edited by Larry L. Rasmussen. Translated by Isabel Best and David Higgins. Supplementary material translated by Douglas W. Stott. DBWE 12. Minneapolis: Fortress, 2009.

———. *Discipleship.* Edited by Geffrey B. Kelly and John Godsey. Translated by Barbara Green and Reinhard Krauss. DBWE 4. Minneapolis: Fortress, 2001.

———. *Ecumenical, Academic, and Pastoral Work, 1931–1932.* Edited by Victoria J. Barnett et al. Translated by Anne Schmidt-Lange et al. DBWE 11. Minneapolis: Fortress, 2012.

———. "Essay About American Protestantism." In *Theological Education Underground, 1937–1940*, edited by Victoria J. Barnett, 438–62. Translated by Victoria J. Barnett et al. Supplementary material translated by Douglas W. Stott. DBWE 15. Minneapolis: Fortress, 2012.

Bibliography

———. *Ethics*. Edited by Clifford J. Green. Translated by Reinhard Krauss et al. DBWE 6. Minneapolis: Fortress, 2005.

———. "Lecture Course: The Nature of the Church (Student Notes)." In *Ecumenical, Academic, and Pastoral Work, 1931-1932*, edited by Victoria J. Barnett et al., 269-332. Translated by Anne Schmidt-Lange et al. DBWE 11. Minneapolis: Fortress, 2012.

———. "Lectures on Christology (Student Notes)." In *Berlin, 1932-1933*, edited by Larry L. Rasmussen, 12:299-360. Translated by Isabel Best and David Higgins. Supplementary material translated by Douglas W. Stott. DBWE 12. Minneapolis: Fortress, 2009.

———. *Letters and Papers from Prison*. Edited by John W. de Gruchy. Translated by Isabel Best et al. DBWE 8. Minneapolis: Fortress, 2010.

———. *"Life Together"; "Prayerbook of the Bible."* Edited by Geffrey B. Kelly. Translated by Daniel W. Eloesch. DBWE 5. Minneapolis: Fortress, 1996.

———. *London, 1933-1935*. Edited by Keith Clements. Translated by Isabel Best. Supplementary material translated by Douglas W. Stott. DBWE 13. Minneapolis: Fortress, 2007.

———. *Sanctorum Communio: A Theological Study of the Sociology of the Church*. Edited by Clifford J. Green. Translated by Reinhard Krauss and Nancy Lukens. DBWE 1 Minneapolis: Fortress, 1998.

———. *Theological Education Underground, 1937-1940*. Edited by Victoria J. Barnett. Translated by Victoria J. Barnett et al. Supplementary material translated by Douglas W. Stott. DBWE 15. Minneapolis: Fortress, 2012.

———. "What Does It Mean to Tell the Truth?" In *Conspiracy and Imprisonment, 1940-1945*, edited by Mark S. Brocker 601-8. Translated by Lisa E. Dahill. Supplementary material translated by Douglas W. Stott. DBWE 16. Minneapolis: Fortress, 2006.

Bonhoeffer, Dietrich, and Maria von Wedemeyer. *Love Letters from Cell 92, 1943-1945*. Edited by Ruth-Alice von Bismarck and Ulrich Kabitz. With a postscript by Eberhard Bethge. Translated by John Brownjohn. London: HarperCollins, 1994.

Bosch, David. "Nothing but a Heresy." In *Apartheid Is a Heresy*, edited by John W. de Gruchy and Charles Villa-Vicencio, 24-38. Grand Rapids: Eerdmans, 1983.

Bradley, W. L. *P. T. Forsyth, The Man and His Work*. London: Independent,1952.

Briggs, D. Roy, *A Covenant Church: Studies in the Polity of the United Congregational Church of Southern Africa in Terms of Its Covenant*. Gaborone, Botswana: Pula, 1996.

Briggs, D. Roy, and Joseph Wing. *The Harvest and the Hope: The Story of Congregationalism in Southern Africa*. Johannesburg, SA: UCCSA, 1970

Brown, Colin. "Soul." In *The New International Dictionary of New Testament Theology*, edited by Colin Brown, 3:676-89. 3 vols. Exeter, UK: Paternoster, 1978.

Brown, Raymond E, *The Gospel According to John*. 2 vols. AB 29-29A. New York: Doubleday, 1966-1970.

Buber, Martin. *I and Thou*. Translated by Ronald Gregor Smith. Edinburgh: T. & T. Clark, 1958.
Burridge, Richard A. *Imitating Jesus: An Inclusive Approach to New Testament Ethics*. Grand Rapids: Eerdmans, 2007.
Burt, Donald X., OSA. *Friendship and Society: An Introduction to Augustine's Practical Philosophy*. Grand Rapids: Eerdmans, 1999.
Busch, Eberhard, *Karl Barth: His Life from Letters and Autobiographical Texts*. Philadelphia: Fortress, 1976.
―――. *Karl Barth: His Life from Letters and Autobiographical Texts*. 1976. Reprint, Eugne, OR: Wipf & Stock, 2005.
Butler, Philip. "Black Theology and Artificial Intelligence." In *CCRAI*, 182–200.
Carson, J. J. G. *Emilie Solomon, 1858–1939*. Cape Town, SA: Juta, 1941.
Chadwick, Owen. *The Victorian Church, Part 1*, 2 vols. London: Black, 1966.
Chesterton, G. K. *Orthodoxy*. With an introduction by Philip Yancey. New York: Image, 2001.
Christofersen, Arthur Fridjof. *Adventuring with God: The Story of the American Board Mission in South Africa*, Durban, SA: Robinson, 1967.
Clements, Keith W. "Dialogue or Confession? Ecumenical Responsibility and the War in Ukraine." *Journal of Anglican Studies* 21 (2023) 246–59.
―――. "Dialogue with the Orthodox World: A Further Journey for Bonhoeffer." In *Bonhoeffer for a New Day: Theology in a Time of Transition*, edited by John W. de Gruchy, 340–52. Grand Rapids: Eerdmans, 1997.
―――. "The Freedom of the Church: Bonhoeffer and the Free Church Tradition." In *Bonhoeffer's Ethics: Old Europe and New Frontiers*, edited by Guy Carter et.al., 155–72. Kampen: Kok Pharos, 1991.
―――. *A Patriotism for Today: Love of Country in Dialogue with the Witness of Dietrich Bonhoeffer*. With a foreword by Eberhard Bethge. Eugene, OR: Wipf & Stock 2011.
Cloete, G. D., and D. J. Smit, eds. *A Moment of Truth: The Confession of the Dutch Reformed Mission Church*. Grand Rapids: Eerdmans, 1984.
Cochrane, Charles N. *Christianity and Classical Culture*. A Galaxy Book. London: Oxford University Press, 1957.
Cochrane, James R., et al., eds. *Living on the Edge: Essays in Honour of Steve de Gruchy, Activist & Theologian*. Pietermaritzburg, SA: Cluster, 2012
Comaroff. Jean, and John Comaroff. *Of Revelation and Revolution: Christianity, Colonialism and Consciousness in South Africa*. Vol. 2, *The Dialectics of Modernity on a South African Frontier*. Chicago: University of Chicago Press, 1997.
Conradie, Ernst M. "Liberation, Reconciliation or Transformation? Revisiting the *Kairos Document* and the *Belhar Confession*." In "The Contested Legacy of the *Kairos Document*." Special issue, *Journal of Theology for Southern Africa* 177 (2023) 103–21.
Cornford, Francis Macdonald. Introduction. In *The Republic of Plato*. Translated with an introduction by Francis Macdconald Cornford, xiii–xxvii. 1941. Reprint, Oxford: Clarendon, 1955.

Cullmann, Oscar. *Christ and Time: The Primitive Christian Conception of Time and History*. With a new introductory chapter. Translated from the German by Floyd V. Filson. Rev. ed. London: SCM, 1962.

———. *Immortality of the Soul or Resurrection of the Dead? The Witness of the New Testament*. Ingersoll Lectures 1955. New York: Macmillan, 1964.

Dalferth, Ingolf U. *The Passion of Possibility: Studies on Kierkegaard's Post-Metaphysical Theology*. Kierkegaard Studies Monograph Series 48. Berlin: de Gruyter, 2023.

Davenport, T. R. H. "The Consolidation of a New Society: The Cape Colony." In *The Oxford History of South Africa*. Vol. 1, *South Africa to 1870*, edited by Monica Wilson and Leonard Thompson, 272–333. Oxford: Clarendon, 1969.

Davies, Horton. *The English Free Churches*. 2nd ed. Home University Library of Modern Knowledge 220. London Oxford University Press, 1963.

De Gruchy, John W. "Anticipating Liberation Theology: Franz Hildebrandt's 'Gospel and Humanitarianism.'" In *El silbo ecuménico del Espíritu: homenaje a José Míguez Bonino en sus 80 años*, edited by Guillermo Hansen, 179–92. Buenos Aires: Institutio Universitario ISEDET, 2005.

———. "Barmen: A Symbol of Contemporary Liberation." In *The Barmen Confession: Papers from the Seattle Assembly*, edited by Hubert G. Locke, 335–62. Toronto Studies in Theology 26. Lewiston, NY: Mellen, 1986.

———. *Being Human: Confessions of a Christian Humanist*. London: SCM, 2006.

———. "Beyers Naudé: South Africa's Bonhoeffer? Celebrating the Centenary of the Birth of Beyers Naudé—1915–2015." *STJ* 1.1 (2014) 79–98.

———. *Bonhoeffer and South Africa: Theology in Dialogue*. Grand Rapids: Eerdmans 1984.

———. "Bonhoeffer in South Africa: An Exploratory Essay." In *Bonhoeffer: Exile and Martyr*, by Eberhard Bethge, 26–42. Edited by John W. de Gruchy. London: Collins, 1975.

———. "Bonhoeffer's Legacy and Kairos-Palestine." *Journal of Theology for Southern Africa* 143 (July 2012) 67–80.

———. *Bonhoeffer's Questions: A Life-Changing Conversation*. Lanham, MD: Fortress Academic, 2019.

———. "Christ Under the Rubble: Bonhoeffer on Aesthetic Existence in the Church as a Sphere of Freedom in a Time of War." *STJ* 10.1 (2024) 1–25.

———. *Christianity and Democracy: Theology for a Just World Order*. Cambridge Studies in Ideology and Religion. Cambridge: Cambridge University Press, 1995.

———. *Christianity and the Modernisation of South Africa, 1867–1936: A Documentary History, Volume II*. Hidden Histories Series. Pretoria: Unisa, 2009.

———. *Christianity, Art, and Transformation: Theological Aesthetics in the Struggle for Justice*. Cambridge: Cambridge University Press, 2001.

———. *The Church Struggle in South Africa*. Grand Rapids: Eerdmans, 1979.

Bibliography

———. *The Church Struggle in South Africa*. 2nd ed. Grand Rapids: Eerdmans, 1986.

———. "The Congregational Way: A Historical Study of the Congregational Doctrine of the Church." BD thesis, Rhodes University, 1960.

———. "Conversion & the Persistence of Colonial Racism." In *Faith Facing Reality: Stirring Up Discussion with Bonhoeffer*, 31–55. Eugene, OR: Cascade Books, 2022.

———. *Daring, Trusting Spirit: Bonhoeffer's Friend Eberhard Bethge*. London: SCM, 2005.

———. "Dietrich Bonhoeffer as Christian Humanist." In *Being Human, Becoming Human: Dietrich Bonhoeffer and Social Thought*, edited by Jens Zimmerman and Brian Gregor, 3–24. Princeton Theological Monograph Series 146. Eugene, OR: Pickwick Publications, 2010.

———. "Dietrich Bonhoeffer, Nelson Mandela and the Dilemma of Violent Resistance in Retrospect." *STJ* 2.1 (2016) 43–60.

———. "The Dynamic Structure of the Church: A Comparative Study of the Ecclesiologies of Karl Barth and Dietrich Bonhoeffer." PhD diss., University of South Africa, 1972.

———. "Ecumenical Dissent from Christendom to Christian Nationalism: The Testimony of a South African Congregationalist dissenter", *STJ*, 11.1 (2025), 1–35."

———. *The End Is Not Yet: Standing Firm in Apocalyptic Times*, Dispatches. Minneapolis: Fortress, 2017.

———. *Faith Facing Reality: Stirring Up Discussion with Bonhoeffer*. Eugene, OR: Cascade Books, 2022.

———. "Fortune and Calamity." In *Letters and Papers from Prison*, edited by John W. de Gruchy, 431–42. Translated by Isabel Best et al. DBWE 8. Minneapolis: Fortress, 2010.

———. *Icons as a Means of Grace*. Cape Town, SA: Lux Verbi, 2011.

———. *I Have Come a Long Way*. Eugene, OR: Cascade Books, 2016.

———. *John Calvin: Christian Humanist and Evangelical Reformer*. Eugene, OR: Cascade Books, 2013.

———. "Kairos Moments and Prophetic Witness: Towards a Prophetic Ecclesiology." *HTS: Theological Studies* 72.4 (2016) 1–7.

———. *Led into Mystery: Faith Seeking Answers in Life and Death*. London: SCM, 2013.

———. *Liberating Reformed Theology: A South African Contribution to an Ecumenical Debate*. Grand Rapids: Eerdmans, 1991.

———. "The Local Church and Racial Identity." MTh thesis, Chicago Theological Seminary, 1964.

———. "On Being a Prophetic Church at *This Kairos* Moment: In Celebration of Albert Nolan; Prophet, Disciple, and Mystic." In "The Contested Legacy of the *Kairos Document*." Special issue, *Journal of Theology for Southern Africa* 177 (2023) 87–102.

———. "The Past." In *Letters and Papers from Prison*, edited by John W. de Gruchy, 418–31. Translated by Isabel Best et al. DBWE 8. Minneapolis: Fortress, 2010.

———. "Providence and the Shapers of History." In *Bonhoeffer and South Africa: Theology in Dialogue*, 47–66. Grand Rapids: Eerdmans, 1984.

———. "Radical Peace-Making: The Challenge of Some Anabaptists." In, *Theology & Violence: The South African Debate*, edited by Charles Villa-Vicencio, 173–85. Johannesburg, SA: Skotaville. 1987.

———. "The Reception and Relevance of Karl Barth in South Africa: Reflections on 'Doing Theology' in South Africa After Sixty Years in Conversation with Barth." *STJ* 5.1 (2019) 11–28.

———. *Reconciliation: Restoring Justice*. Hulsean Lectures 2002. London: SCM, 2002.

———. "Remembering a Legacy." In *The London Missionary Society in Southern Africa: Historical Essays on the LMS in Southern Africa, 1799–1999*, edited by John W. de Gruchy, 1–6. Cape Town, SA: David Philip, 1999; copublished Athens: Ohio University Press, 2000.

———. "Retrieving the Soul: Understanding the Soul as Complex, Dynamic and Relational." *Journal of Theology in Southern Africa* 149 (July 2014) 56–69.

———. "A Short History of the Christian Institute." In *Resistance and Hope: South African Essays in Honour of Beyers Naudé*, edited by Charles Villa-Vicencio and John W. de Gruchy, 14–26. Grand Rapids: Eerdmans, 1985.

———. *A Theological Odyssey: My Life in Writing*, Beyers Naudé Centre Series on Public Theology 7. Stellenbosch, SA: Sun Press, 2014.

———. *This Monastic Moment: The War of the Spirit & the Rule of Love*. Eugene, OR: Cascade Books, 2021.

———. "Wisdom & the Threat of Scientism and Soulless Technology." In *Faith Facing Reality:Stirring Up Discussion with Bonhoeffer*, 79–103. Eugene, OR: Cascade Books, 2022.

De Gruchy, John W., and Bruckner de Villiers, eds. *The Message in Perspective: A Book About "A Message to the People of South Africa."* Johannesburg, SA: SACC, 1969.

De Gruchy, John W., and Steve de Gruchy. *The Church Struggle in South Africa*. 3rd, 25th anniversary ed. London: SCM, 2004.

De Gruchy, John W., and Charles Villa-Vicencio, eds. *Apartheid Is a Heresy*. Grand Rapids: Eerdmans, 1983.

De Gruchy, Steve, ed. *Changing Frontiers: The Mission Story of the United Congregational Church of Southern Africa*. Gaborone, Botswana: Pula, 1999.

———. "Dissenting Calvinism: Reflections on the Congregational Witness in South Africa as Part of the Wider Reformed Tradition." *Theologia Viatorum* 28.1(2004) 1–23.

———. "From *Kairos* to Belhar: On Being Church in a Time of AIDS." In *Keeping Body and Soul Together: Reflections by Steve de Gruchy on Theology and Development*, edited by Beverley Haddad, 242–53. Pietermaritzburg, SA: Cluster, 2015.

———."Locating *The Church Struggle in South Africa* in the Wider Historiography of the Church in South Africa." In *The Church Struggle in South Africa*, by John W. de Gruchy and Steve de Gruchy, xxvii–xxx. 3rd, 25th anniversary ed. London: SCM, 2004.

———. "A Remarkable Life: The Story of Joseph Wing." In *Spirit Undaunted: The Life and Legacy of Joseph Wing*, edited by Steve de Gruchy and Desmond van der Walter, 1–126. Pietermaritzburg, SA: Cluster, 2005.

De Klerk, W. A. *The Puritans in Africa: A History of Afrikanerdom*. Pelican Books. Harmondsworth, UK: Penguin, 1976.

Delio, Ilia. "Transhumanism and Transcendence." In *CCRAI*, 131–47.

Denis, Philippe. "The Historical Roots of Southern African Congregationalism." In *Living on the Edge: Essays in Honour of Steve de Gruchy, Activist & Theologian*, edited by James R. Cochrane et al., 303–19. Pietermaritzburg, SA: Cluster, 2012.

Dihle, Albert. "ψυχή." In *TDNT* 9:637–58.

Dodd, C.H. *The Apostolic Preaching and Its Developments*. London: Hodder & Stoughton, 1936.

Dorobantu, Marius. "Artificial Intelligence and Christianity." In *CCRAI*, 88–108.

Dunn, James D. G. *Christology in the Making: A New Testament Inquiry into the Origins of the Doctrine of the Incarnation*. London: SCM, 1980.

Du Plessis, J. *A History of Christian Missions in South Africa*. Cape Town, SA: Struik, 1965

Durand, J. J. F. "Afrikaner Piety and Dissent." In *Resistance and Hope: South African Essays in Honour of Beyers Naudé*, edited by Charles Villa-Vicencio and John W. de Gruchy 39–51. Grand Rapids: Eerdmans, 1985.

Durnbaugh, Donald F. *The Believers' Church: The History and Character of Radical Protestantism*. New York: Macmillan, 1968.

Du Sautoy, Marcus. *Blueprints: How Mathematics Shapes Creativity*. London: 4th Estate, 2025.

Eagleton, Terry. *Culture*. New Haven: Yale University Press, 2016.

Erlank, Natasha. "Jane and John Philip: Partnership, Usefulness and Sexuality in the Service of God." In *The London Missionary Society in Southern Africa: Historical Essays on the LMS in Southern Africa, 1799–1999*, edited by John W. de Gruchy, 82–98, Cape Town, SA: David Philip, 1999; copublished in Athens: Ohio University Press, 2000.

Etherington, Norman. "Kingdoms of This World and the Next: Christian Beginnings Among Zulu and Swazi." In *Christianity in South Africa: A Political, Social & Cultural History*, edited by Richard Elphick and Rodney Davenport, 89–106. Cape Town, SA: David Philip, 1997.

Ferguson, George P. *CUSA: The Story of the Congregational Union of South Africa*. Paarl, SA: Fischer, 1940.

Feuerbach, Ludwig. *The Essence of Christianity*. Translated by George Eliot. With an introductory essay by Karl Barth and a foreword by H. Richard Niebuhr. Harper Torchbooks. The Library of Religion and Culture. New York: Harper & Row, 1957.

Floyd, Samuel A., Jr. *The Power of Black Music: Interpreting Its History from Africa to the United States* New York: Oxford University Press, 1995.

Foerst, Anne. "Cog, a Humancid Robot, and the Question of the Image of God." *Zygon: Journal of Religion and Science* 33.1 (March 1998) 91–111.

Forrester, Duncan B. *On Human Worth: A Christian Vindication of Equality*. London: SCM, 2001.

Forsyth, P. T. *Congregationalism and Reunion*. London: Independent, 1952.

———. *Faith, Freedom and the Future*. London: Independent, 1912. Reprint, 1955.

———. *The Justification of God: Lectures for War-Time on a Christian Theodicy*. London: Independent, 1943.

———. *The Person and Place of Jesus Christ*. 8th ed. London: Independent, 1955.

———. *Socialism, the Church and the Poor*. London: Hodder & Stoughton, 1908.

Francis, Pope. *Hope: The Autobiography*. London: Penguin, 2025.

Frend, W. H. C. *The Rise of Christianity*. Philadelphia: Fortress, 1984

Fry, Stephen. *Odyssey: Can a Hero Find His Way Home?* London: Penguin, 2024.

Gadamer, Hans-Georg. "The Play of Art." In *The Relevance of the Beautiful and Other Essays*, edited with an introduction by Robert Bernascon, 123–30. Translated by Nicholas Walker. Cambridge: Cambridge University Press, 1986.

———. *Truth and Method*. Translation revised by Joel Weinsheimer and Donald G. Marshall. 2nd rev ed. New York: Crossroad, 1989.

Ganoczy, Alexandre. *The Young Calvin*. Translated by David Foxgrover and Wade Provo. Philadelphia: Westminster, 1987.

Gilbert, Jack. "A Brief for the Defense." In *Collected Poems*, 317. New York: Knopf, 2012.

Gorringe, Timothy J. *Karl Barth: Against Hegemony*. Christian Theology in Context, Oxford: Oxford University Press, 1999.

Grant, John W. *Free Churchmanship in England 1870–1940, with Special Reference to Congregationalism*. London: Independent, 1955.

Grant, Robert M. *Augustus to Constantine: The Thrust of the Christian Movement into the Roman World*. London: Collins, 1971.

Gregory the Theologian. "Letter 101 to Cledonius." In *Christ: Through the Nestorian Controversy*, edited by Mark DelCogliano, 388–98. The Cambridge Edition of Early Christian Writings 3. Cambridge: Cambridge University Press. 2022.

Green, Clifford J. *Bonhoeffer: A Theology of Sociality*. Rev. ed. Grand Rapids: Eerdmans, 1999.

BIBLIOGRAPHY

Grillmeier, Alois. *Christ in Christian Tradition*. Vol. 1, *From the Apostolic Age to Chalcedon*. Translated by John Bowden. Atlanta: John Knox, 1975.

———. *Christ in Christian Tradition*. Vol. 2, Part 1, *From Chalcedon to Justinian*. Translated by Pauline Allen and John Cawte. Atlanta: John Knox, 1987.

Gritsch, Eric C. *Thomas Müntzer: A Tragedy of Errors*. Minneapolis: Fortress, 1989.

Handy, Robert T. *A Christian America: Protestant Hopes and Historical Realities*. New York: Oxford University Press, 1971.

Harnack Adolf von. *The Mission and Expansion of Christianity in the First Three Centuries*. Translated by James Moffatt. Harper Torchbooks. New York: Harper, 1962.

———. *What Is Christianity?* Translated by Thomas Bailey Saunders. Twentieth Century Religious Thought 1. Philadelphia: Fortress, 1986.

Harari, Yuval Noah. *Nexus: A Brief History of Information Networks from the Stone Age to AI*. London: Fern, 2024.

Hebblethwaite, Brian. "Soul." In *The Oxford Companion to Christian Thought*, edited by Adrian Hastings et al., 681–83. Oxford: Oxford University Press, 2000.

Heisenberg, Werner. *Physics & Philosophy: The Revolution in Modern Science*. London: Penguin 1990.

Hershberger, Guy F., ed. *The Recovery of the Anabaptist Vision*. 1957. Reprint, Eugene, OR: Wipf & Stock, 2001.

Hewson, Leslie A., ed. *The Cottesloe Consultation: The Report of the Consultation Among South African Member Churches of the World Council of Churches, 7-14 Dec. 1960 at Cottesloe, Johannesburg*. Johannesburg, SA: n.p., 1961.

Hildebrandt, Franz. "Gospel and Humanitarianism." DPhil diss., Cambridge University, 1941.

———. "An Oasis of Freedom." In *I Knew Dietrich Bonhoeffer: Reminiscences by His Friends*, edited by Wolf-Dieter Zimmerman and Ronald Gregor Smith, 38–40. Translated by Kathe Gregor Smith. London: Collins, 1966.

Hinchliff, Peter. *The Anglican Church in South Africa*. London: Darton, Longman & Todd, 1963.

Hill, Edmund, OP. Introduction. In *The Trinity*, by Augustine, 18–59. Edited by John E. Rotelle. Translated, with introduction and notes, by Edmund Hill, OP. The Works of Saint Augustine, pt. 1, vol. 5. Brooklyn: New City, 1991.

Hofstadter, Douglas R. *Gödel, Escher, Bach: An Eternal Golden Braid*. 20th ann. ed. New York: Basic Books, 1999.

Huber, Wolfgang. "What Does It Mean to Tell the Truth? Bonhoeffer in a Digital Era." In *Bonhoeffer and the Responsibility for a Coming Generation: Doing Theology in a Time Out of Joint*, edited by Robert Vosloo et al., 28–39. T. & T. Clark New Studies in Bonhoeffer's Theology and Ethics. London: T. & T. Clark, 2024.

Jansen, Alan Lance. "The Influence of Fundamentalism on Evangelicalism in South Africa with Special Reference to the Role of Plymouth Brethrenism amongst the Cape Coloured Population." PhD. diss., University of Cape Town, SA, 2002.

Jenson, Robert W. *America's Theologian: A Recommendation of Jonanthan Edwards*. New York: Oxford University Press, 1988.

Kairos Theologians. *The Kairos Document*. Johannesburg: Institute for Contextual Theology, 1986.

Karis, Thomas G., et al., eds. *From Protest to Challenge: A Documentary History of African Politics in South Africa, 1882–1990*, Vol. 5, *Nadir and Resurgence, 1964–1979*, edited by Thomas G. Karis and Gail M. Gerhart. Stanford: Hoover Institution Press, 1997.

Kaylor, Brian, and Beau Underwood. *Baptizing America: How Mainline Protestants Helped Build Christian Nationalism*. Des Peres, MO: Chalice, 2024.

Keegan, Timothy J. *Dr Philip's Empire: One Man's Struggle for Justice in Nineteenth-Century South Africa*. Cape Town, SA: Zebra, 2016.

Keet, B. B. *Whither, South Africa?* Stellenbosch: University Publishers & Booksellers, 1956.

Kelly, J. N. D. *Early Christian Creeds*. London: Longmans, 1950.

———. *Early Christian Doctrines*. 4th ed. London: Black, 1968.

Kierkegaard, Søren. *The Journals of Søren Kierkegaard: A Selection*. Edited and translated by Alexander Dru. Fontana Books. Fontana Religious. London: Collins, 1958.

———. *Kierkegaard's Attack upon "Christendom," 1854–1855*. Translated, with an introduction, by Walter Lowrie. Princeton: Princeton University Press, 1944.

Kingsnorth, Paul. *Against the Machine: On the Unmasking of Humanity*. New York: Thesis, 2025.

Kleinknecht, Herman. "πνεῦμά." In *TDNT* 6:332–59.

Klinger, Elmar. "Soul," In *Encyclopaedia of Theology: A Concise Sacramentum Mundi*, edited by Karl Rahner, 1615–18. London: Burns & Oates, 1975.

Kohn, Linda T., et al., eds. *To Err Is Human: Building a Safer Health System*. Washington, DC: National Academy Press, 2000.

Krahn, Cornelius. *Dutch Anabaptism: Origin, Spread, Life and Thought, 1450–1600*. The Hague: Nijhoff, 1968.

Kurzweil, Ray. *The Age of Spiritual Machines: When Computers Exceed Human Intelligence*. New York: Viking, 1999.

LaCugna, Catherine Mowry. *God for Us: The Trinity and Christian Life*. San Francisco: HarperSanFrancisco, 1991.

Leith, John H., ed. *Creeds of the Churches*. Rev. ed. Oxford: Blackwell, 1973.

Loewenich, Walther von. *Luther's Theology of the Cross*. Translated by Herbert J. A. Bouma Belfast: Christian Journals, 1976.

———. *Luther's Theology of the Cross*. Translated by Herbert J. A. Bouma Minneapolis: Augsburg, 1976.

Lonergan, Bernard J. F. *Insight: A Study of Human Understanding*. Rev. students ed. London: Darton, Longman & Todd, 1958.

BIBLIOGRAPHY

Longenecker, Richard N. *Galatians*, Word Biblical Commentary 41. Dallas: Word, 1990.

Lowerie, Walter. *Kierkegaard*. Vol. 2. Harper Torchbooks. Cloister Library. New York: Harper, 1962.

Lull, Timothy F., ed. *Martin Luther's Basic Theological Writings*. With a foreword by Jaroslav Pelikan. Minneapolis: Fortress, 1989.

Lukens, Nancy, and Renate Bethge. "'By Powers of Good': Bonhoeffer's Last Poem." In *Who Am I? Bonhoeffer's Theology Through His Poetry*, edited by Bernd Wannenwetsch, 71–90. T. & T. Clark Theology. London: T. & T. Clark, 2009.

Luthuli, Albert. *Let My People Go: An Autobiography*. Introduced by Charles Hooper. London: Collins, 1962.

MacIntyre, Alisdair. *After Virtue: A Study in Moral Theory*. Notre Dame, IN: University of Notre Dame Press, 1981.

Manning, Bernard Lord. *Essays in Orthodox Dissent*. London: Independent, 1939.

———. *The Hymns of Wesley and Watts*. London: Epworth, 1988

Marsden, George M. *Fundamentalism and American Culture: The Shaping of Twentieth Century Evangelicalism, 1870–1925*. A Galaxy Book. New York: Oxford University Press, 1982.

Marsh, Charles. *Strange Glory: A Life of Dietrich Bonhoeffer*. New York: Knopf, 2014.

Matthews, Z. K. "The Road from Nonviolence to Violence." In *From Protest to Challenge: A Documentary History of African Politics in South Africa, 1882–1990*, edited by Thomas G. Karis et al. Vol. 5, *Nadir and Resurgence, 1964–1979*, edited by Thomas G. Karis and Gail M. Gerhart, 347–55. Stanford: Hoover Institution Press, 1997.

McCrummen, Stephanie. "The Army of God Comes Out of the Shadows." *Atlantic*, February 2025. https://www.theatlantic.com/magazine/archive/2025/02/new-apostolic-reformation-christian-movement-trump/681092/.

McGilchrist, Iain. *The Master and His Emissary: The Divided Brain and the Making of the Western World*. New Haven: Yale University Press, 2009.

McNeil, John T. *The History and Character of Calvinism*. New York: Oxford University Press, 1954.

Mead, George H. *Mind, Self & Society: From the Standpoint of a Social Behaviorist*. Edited with introduction, by Charles W. Morris. Chicago: University of Chicago Press, 1934.

Miller, Perry. *Jonathan Edwards*. A Meridian Book. Cleveland, OH: World, 1963.

Mokoena, K. K. "A Holistic Ubuntu Artificial Intelligence Ethics Approach in South Africa." *Verbum et Ecclesia* 45.1 (2024). DOI:10.4102/ve.v45i1.3100.

———. "Towards an Ubuntu/Botho Ethics of Technology." PhD diss., University of Pretoria, 2023.

BIBLIOGRAPHY

Moltmann, Jürgen. *The Church in the Power of the Spirit: A Contribution to Messianic Ecclesiology*. Translated by Margaret Kohl. London: SCM, 1977.

———. *The Crucified God*. Translated by R. A. Wilson and John Bowden. SCM Classics. London: SCM, 1974.

———. *On Human Dignity: Political Theology and Ethics*. Translated and with an introduction by M. Douglas Meeks. Philadelphia: Fortress, 1984.

Moodie, T. Dunbar. *The Rise of Afrikanerdom: Power, Apartheid, and the Afrikaner Civil Religion*. Perspectives on Southern Africa 11. Berkeley: University of California Press, 1975.

Moule, C. F. D. *The Origin of Christology*. Cambridge: Cambridge University Press, 1977.

Mubeen, Junaid. *Mathematical Intelligence: What We Have That Machines Don't*. London: Profile Books, 2024

Mumford, Lewis. *Technics and Civilization*. London: Routledge., 1934.

Munson James. *The Nonconformists: In Search of a Lost Culture*. London: SPCK, 1991.

Nakashima, George. *The Soul of a Tree*. 1st paperback ed. Distributed in the U.S. by Kodansha through Harper & Row. Tokyo: Kodansha, 1988.

Ndungane, Njongonkulu. Foreword. In *Spirit Undaunted: The Life and Legacy of Joseph Wing*, edited by Steve de Gruchy and Desmond van der Walter, vii–viii. Pietermaritzburg, SA: Cluster, 2005

Niebuhr, Reinhold. *The Self and the Dramas of History*. New York: Scribner, 1955.

Nieder-Heitmann, Jan. "Christendom at the Cape: A Critical Examination of the Early Formation of the Dutch Reformed Church." PhD diss., University of Cape Town, SA, 2007.

Nietzsche, Friedrich. *The Will to Power*. Edited, with commentary, by Walter Kaufmann. Translated by Walter Kaufmann and R. J. Hollingdale. A Vintage Giant. New York: Random House, 1968.

Oduro, Thomas A., et al., eds. *Unless a Grain of Wheat: A Story of Friendship Between African Independent Churches and North American Mennonites*. Carlisle, UK: Langham Creative Projects, 2021.

Olson, Parmy. *Supremacy: AI, ChatGPT and the Race That Will Change the World*. London: Macmillan, 2024.

Ord, Toby. *The Precipice: Existential Risk and the Future of Humanity*. London: Bloomsbury, 2020.

Pangritz, Andreas. *The Polyphony of Life: Bonhoeffer's Theology of Music*. Edited by John W. de Gruchy and John Morris. Translated by Robert Steiner. Eugene, OR: Cascade Books, 2019.

Pelikan, Jaroslav. *The Christian Tradition*. Vol. 2, *The Spirit of Eastern Christendom (600–1700)*. Chicago: University of Chicago Press, 1974.

Porteous, Rebecca Baer. "Seeking the Dawn: A Critical Reflection upon and Response to the Theology of John de Gruchy." PhD diss., Duke University,1998.

Postman, Neil. *Amusing Ourselves to Death: Public Discourse in the Age of Show Business.* New York: Penguin, 1985.

Prüller-Jagenteufel, Gunter. "Dietrich Bonhoeffer—Pacifist and Resistance Fighter: A Dialectic with a Current Relevance." In *Echoes of Bonhoeffer: The Political Dimensions of Reconciliation and Interfaith Encounter*, edited by Zeina M. Barakat and Thies Münchow, 61–68. Reconciliation and Conflict Resolution 6. Freiburg: WBG Academic, 2025.

Ratzinger, Joseph. "The Dignity of the Human Person." In *Commentary on the Documents of Vatican II*, edited by Herbert Vorgrimler. Vol. 5, *Pastoral Constitution on the Church in the Modern World*, 115–63. New York: Herder, 1969.

———. "The Reality of Life After Death: Recentiores Episcoporum Synodi, 11 May 1979." In *Vatican II: More Postconciliar Documents*, edited by Austin Flannery, 500–504. Vatican Collection 2. Grand Rapids: Eerdmans, 1982.

Rodgers John H. *The Theology of P. T. Forsyth: The Cross of Christ and the Revelation of God*, London: Independent, 1965.

Rolf, Veronica Mary. *Julian's Gospel: Illuminating the Life & Revelations of Julian of Norwich.* Maryknoll, NY: Orbis, 2013.

Rumscheidt, H. Martin. *Revelation and Theology: An Analysis of the Barth-Harnack Correspondence of 1923.* Monograph Supplements to the Scottish Journal of Theology. Cambridge: Cambridge University Press, 1972.

Runciman, Steven. *The Eastern Schism: A Study of the Papacy and the Eastern Churches During the XIth and XIIth Centuries.* Oxford: Clarendon, 1955.

Ryle, Gilbert. *The Concept of Mind.* Senior Series. London: Hutchinson's University Library, 1949.

Saayman, Willem. "Rebels and Prophets: Afrikaners Against the System." In *Resistance and Hope: South African Essays in Honour of Beyers Naudé*, edited by Charles Villa-Vicencio and John W. de Gruchy, 52–60. Grand Rapids: Eerdmans, 1985.

Schleiermacher, Friedrich. *The Christian Faith.* Translated by H. R. Mackintosh and J. S. Stewart. Edinburgh: T. & T. Clark, 1928. Reprint, 1968.

Schmemann, Alexander. *For the Life of the World.* New York: National Student Christian Federation, 1963.

Schweizer, Eduard. "σάρχ." In *TDNT* 7:124–51.

———. "σῶμά." In *TDNT* 7:1057–94.

Sifton, Elisabeth, and Fritz Stern. *No Ordinary Men: Dietrich Bonhoeffer and Hans von Dohnanyi, Resisters Against Hitler in Church and State.* New York Review Books Collections. New York: New York Review Books, 2013.

Singler, Beth. "The Anthropology and Sociology of Religion and AI." In *CCRAI*, 222–30.

Singler, Beth, and Fraser Watts, eds. *Cambridge Companion to Religion and Artificial Intelligence (CCRAI).* Cambridge Companions to Religion. Cambridge: Cambridge University Press, 2024.

Slane, Craig J. *Bonhoeffer as Martyr: Social Responsibility and Modern Christian Commitment.* Grand Rapids: Brazos, 2004.

BIBLIOGRAPHY

Smith, Ronald Gregor. Editor's Foreword. In *Against the Stream: Shorter Post-War Writings, 1946–52*, by Karl Barth, 7–11. Edited and translated by Ronald Gregor Smith. London: SCM, 1954.

Stählin, Gustav. "Φιλέω." In *TDNT* 9:113–71.

Stevenson, J., ed. *A New Eusebius*. SPCK Large Paperbacks 1. London: SPCK, 1957.

Suderman, Andrew G. "The Character and Potential Pitfalls of Prophetic Theology: An Appreciatively Critical Look at Fr. Albert Nolan." In "The Contested Legacy of the *Kairos Document*." Special issue, *Journal of Theology for Southern Africa* 177 (2023) 68–86.

Suleyman, Mustafa, with Michael Bhaskar. *The Coming Wave: Technology, Power, and the Twenty-First Century's Greatest Dilemma*. New York: Crown, 2023.

Sundkler, Bengt G. M. *Bantu Prophets in South Africa*. Missionary Research Series 14. Lutterworth Library 32. London: Lutterworth, 1948.

Sykes, S. W. "P.T. Forsyth." In *The Modern Theologians*, edited by David F. Ford, 231–35. 2nd ed. Oxford: Blackwell, 1997.

Taylor, Charles. *A Secular Age*. Cambridge: Belknap, 2007.

Templin, J. Alton. *Ideology on a Frontier: The Theological Foundation of Afrikaner Nationalism, 1652–1910*. Contributions in Intercultural and Comparative Studies 11. Westport, CT: Greenwood, 1984.

Thomas Aquinas. *Summa Theologiae: A Concise Translation*. Edited by Timothy McDermott. Westminster, MD: Christian Classics, 1989.

Torrance, Thomas F. *Theological Science*. Oxford: Oxford University Press, 1978.

Tutu, Desmond. "God's Dream." In *Waging Peace II: Vision and Hope for the 21st Century*, edited by David Krieger and Frank K. Kelly, n.p. Chicago: Noble, 1992.

Vernon, Mark. *Awake! William Blake and the Power of the Imagination*. London: Hurst, 2025.

Villa-Vicencio, Charles, and John W. de Gruchy. *Resistance and Hope: South African Essays in Honour of Beyers Naudé*. Grand Rapids: Eerdmans, 1985

Villa-Vicencio, Charles, and Peter Grassow, *Christianity and the Colonisation of South Africa, A Documentary History, 1487–1883, Volume I*. Hidden Histories Series. Pretoria: Unisa, 2009.

Walker, Williston. *The Creeds and Platforms of Congregationalism*. With an introduction by Douglas Horton. Boston: Pilgrim, 1960.

Wallis, Jim. *The Soul of Politics: A Practical and Prophetic Vision for Change*. New York: New City, 1994.

Walsh, Sylvia. *Living Poetically: Kierkegaard's Existential Aesthetics*. Literature and Philosophy. University Park: Pennsylvania State University Press, 1994.

Wanamaker, Charles A. *The Epistles to the Thessalonians: A Commentary on the Greek Text*. NIGTC. Grand Rapids: Eerdmans 1990.

Wannenwetsch, Bernd, ed. *Who Am I? Bonhoeffer's Theology Through His Poetry*. T. & T. Clark Theology. London: T. & T. Clark, 2009.

BIBLIOGRAPHY

Ware, Kallistos. *The Orthodox Way.* Mowbray's Popular Christian Paperbacks. London: Mowbray, 1979.

Williams, George H. Introduction. In *The Radical Reformation*, xxii–xxxi. Philadelphia: Westminster, 1962.

———. *The Radical Reformation.* Philadelphia: Westminster, 1962.

Williams, Reggie L. *Bonhoeffer's Black Jesus: Harlem Renaissance Theology and an Ethics of Resistance.* Waco, TX: Baylor University Press, 2014.

Williams, Rowan. *Arius: Heresy and Tradition.* 2nd ed. London: SCM, 2001.

———. *On Christian Theology.* Challenges in Contemporary Theology. Oxford: Blackwell, 2000.

———. *Passions of the Soul.* London: Bloomsbury Continuum, 2024.

———. *The Way of St Benedict.* London: Bloomsbury, 2020.

Wolterstorff, Nicholas. *Journey Toward Justice: Personal Encounters in the Global South.* Grand Rapids: Baker Academic, 2013.

Young, Josiah Ulysses, III. *No Difference in the Fare: Dietrich Bonhoeffer and the Problem of Racism.* Grand Rapids: Eerdmans, 1998.

Zijpp, N. van der. "The Early Dutch Anabaptists," in *The Recovery of the Anabaptist* Vision, 69–82.

Zimmermann, Jens. *Incarnational Humanism: A Philosophy of Culture for the Church in the World.* Strategic Initiatives in Evangelical Theology. Downers Grove, IL: IVP Academic, 2012.

Index of Names

Alexander of Alexandria, 30
Aristotle, 40
Arius, 29
Athanasius, 32
Augustine of Hippo, 14, 33, 46, 55, 74–75

Barth, Karl, ix, 12–13, 16–17, 26–7, 42, 44, 79
Bax, Douglas S., 26
Bernard of Clairvaux, 48
Bethge, Dietrich, 48, 72
Bethge, Eberhard, xii, 15, 37, 39, 41, 43, 46, 48, 50–51, 54–56, 85–86
Bethge, Renate, xii, 37, 86
Biko, Steve, 16
Blake, William, 84
Boesak, Allan, 27
Bonhoeffer, Karl Friedrich, 76
Brown, Basil, 12–15
Bullinger, Heinrich, 17
Burnett, Bill, 16

Calvin, John, 14
Charlemagne, 87
Chesterton, G. K., 33
Clements, Keith W., xii
Cromwell, Oliver, 17
Constantine, 29

Dalferth, Ingolf, 47

Damien, Peter, 38–39
Damien of Molokoi, 39
Dante, Alighieri, 38
Darby, John, 12
de Blank, Joost, 15
Descartes, René, 75
de Gruchy, Steve, 21–23, 27, 65, 78
Denis, Phillippe, 5
Dohnanyi, Hans von, 44

Eagleton, Terry, 68
Edwards, Jonanthan, 19
Eusebius of Caesarea, 29

Feuerbach, Ludwig, 66
Forsyth, P. T., 16–17, 20, 32
Francis, Pope, 34, 58
Francis of Assisi, 38
Fry, Stephen, 66–67

Gandhi, Mahatma, 23
Gregory of Nazianzus, 64

Harnack, Adolf von, 13, 42, 44, 75, 78–79
Harari, Yuval Noah, 58, 78
Hebblethwaite, Peter, 76
Heisenberg, Werner, 76
Hildebrandt, Franz, 23, 54
Hitler, Adolf, 8, 23–24, 26, 83
Hofstadter, Douglas, 58
Huber, Wolfgang, 77, 80, 87

Index of Names

Huxley, Julian, 68

Irenaeus, 64

Jackson, Mahalia, 77
Julian of Norwich, 73

Keet, B.B., 14–15
Kierkegaard, Søren, 40–41, 45, 47, 56

Lassere, Jean, 23
Luther, Martin, 17, 31, 34, 48, 85
Lonergan, Bernard J. F., 53
Luthuli, Albert, 24

Manning, Bernard Lord, 34
Marsh, Charles, 53–54
Melancthon, Philip, 17
Menno, Simon, 18
Merton, Thomas, 48
Müntzer, Thomas, 18
Moltmann, Jürgen, 55
Mubeen, Junaid, 61
Mumford, Lewis, 67

Nakashima, George, 77
Naudé, Beyers, 15–16, 21, 51
Niebuhr, Reinhold, 42, 75
Nietzsche, Friedrich, 68, 71, 81
Nolan, Albert, 27

Olsen, Regine, 56
Ord, Toby, 58

Philip, Jane, 25, 35, 50

Philip, John, 9–11, 19–20, 25, 35, 50
Plato, 59
Poelchau, Harald, 86
Postman, Neil, 54

Read, John, 10
Ryle, Gilbert, 74

Savonarola, Girolama, 12
Schleiermacher, Friedrich, 44
Schmemann, Alexander, 34
Schubert, Franz, 54
Singler, Beth, 61
Sellars, Peter, 72
Solomon, Saul, 8–9
Solomon, Emilie, 10
Somerset, Charles, 9–10

Taylor, Charles, 45
Theodosius, 6, 30
Thomas Aquinas, 77
Trump, Donald, 3
Tutu, Desmond, 70
Turing, Alan, 62

Wallis, Jim, 77
Wannenwetsch, Bernd, 49
Ware, Kallistos, 33
Wedemeyer, Maria von, 86
Wilberforce, William, 10
Williams, Rowan, 31, 38, 75, 81
Wesley, John, 7, 10, 19
Wing, Joseph, 20, 25

Zinzendorf, Nikolaus, 10
Zwingli, Ulrich, 17

Index of Subjects

Abyssinian Baptist Church, Harlem, 43, 50
Acedia, 85
Act of Emancipation (1839), 10
Act of Uniformity (1603), 6
aesthetic
  creativity, 51
  existence, 41, 42, 46–47, 49, 52, 54, 56, 62–63, 81
  judgment, 53
aestheticism, 40
African American, 24, 43, 77
African Church, 20, 26
African Independent Churches, 21
African National Congress, 24–25, 28
Afrikaner Republics, 26
"After Ten Years" (Bonhoeffer), 1, 81
Against the Stream (Barth), 18, 79
algorithms, 57, 64, 78
American Board Mission, 19
Anabaptist/ism, 17–18, 20, 24
Anglican (see also Church of England), 11, 26, 54
apartheid (see church struggle), xi, 3, 15–16, 20–1, 26, 70
  armed struggle against, 24, 26, 27
  crime against humanity, 70–71

heresy of, 27–28, 32, 51
apocalyptic times, 29
Arianism, 29
art, 51–54, 63
artificial intelligence, 58, 60,-2, 64, 66–67, 69, 76
artificial general intelligence, xii, 41, 58–64, 68–71, 76–77, 79, 81
  Microsoft CoPilot, 62, 63, 70
  digital immortality, 71
  power of, 59, 68–9
  technological singularity, 59
Attack on Christendom (Kierkegaard), 13

baptism, 11–12, 18
body (*soma*), 73–5
body-mind dualism, 74
Brain, 63
  left hemisphere, 64
  right hemisphere, 65

Calvinism (see also Reformed), 13–14, 17
Catholic, 8, 12, 14, 34, 51
celibacy, 46
Christendom (see dissent), 12–13, 21, 33, 35, 45, 48, 51, 59, 62, 80
  European, 19
  Orthodox, 29

Index of Subjects

Protestant, 8, 14, 17–18, 33
Puritan, 19
Christian
  fundamentalism, 12, 14, 17, 61
  nationalism, 10, 12, 14, 22, 30, 60
  worldliness, 46–47
  year, 85
  Zionism, 12
Christian Council of South Africa, 15
Christian Institute, 15–16
"Christians and Heathen" (Bonhoeffer), 39
Christology (see Jesus Christ), 31
  Bonhoeffer's, 41, 91
Church (see community, ecclesiology, church struggle) 6, 13, 16, 17, 29, 30, 41
  as new humanity, 80
  as fellowship of friends, 55
  as prophetic, 48
  as sphere of freedom, xi, 41, 42, 47, 49–50, 52, 62, 79, 81
  colonialism, 9, 25
  confessing (see church struggle)
  ecumenical, 5, 6, 14, 20, 28, 33, 35, 79
  life of, xi, 17, 54–55, 62–63, 79, 81
  membership, 32
  mission of, 48–49, 79, 80
  for others, 31, 47, 79
  polity, 17, 28–29
  renewal, 48
  Separatist, 21
  theology, 28
  unity, 32
  witness, 33, 35, 80
Church of England, 6–9
Church Struggle
  German, xi, 23, 27–28, 31, 38, 43–45, 54
  South Africa, xi, 2, 16, 20–22, 26–27

Church of the Union, 51
Cog, 62
colonialism, 60
  data colonization, 60
common good, ix, 61–62, 68, 71, 77, 79
Community of the Resurrection, Mirfield, 54
Confessions of faith (see also Creeds), 32–33
Congregational/ism, 5–6, 35
  New England, 14, 19
  polity, 9, 25
Congregational Union of South Africa 10, 25
Consciousness, 58, 67, 73, 79, 82
  transformation of, 67, 69, 81
Conscientious objection, 20, 23, 27
Cottesloe Consultation, 15–16
Council of Constantinople, 30
Council of Nicaea, 29–30, 35–36
creativity (see aesthetic existence, art), 53, 63–64
  artificial, 63
creeds, 32–33
cross
  power of, 66
  theologia crucis 31
culture, 8, 44
  classical, 50
  modern, 8

death, 54, 65, 78, 84
democracy, 20
  transition to, 22, 28
desire
  for God, 40
  for transcendence, 68
deus ex machina, 66
Diet of Speyer (1529) (see Protestant), 17–18
discipleship, 18
  cost of, 24, 40–41, 46–47

Index of Subjects

Discipleship (Bonhoeffer), 23–24, 43, 46–47
disciplina arcanum, 48
dispensationalism, 12
Dissent, xi, 5, 9, 12, 23, 26, 33–35, 44, 48, 82
   Afrikaner, 13, 15
   Catholic, 34
   Congregational, 9, 10–11, 17
   Orthodox, 29, 34
   Radical, 17
   Reformed, 13
Dr. Strangelove, 72
Dutch East India Company, 7
Dutch Reformed Church, 7, 14
Dutch Reformed Mission Church, 27

Eastern Orthodoxy, 30, 33, 34
ecumenical (see church)
Ecumenical Movement (see World Council of Churches), 20, 43
Education, 7, 61
empathy, x, 63, 65, 78
Enlightenment, 45, 51, 73
environment, 68
ethical person, 38
Ethics (Bonhoeffer), 43, 51–52
eugenics, 68
evangelical, 10–11, 14, 35, 43
Evangelical Revival, 7, 19
Evangelical Voluntary Union, 8

faith (see also confessions) ix, 18, 23–24, 28–29, 39, 49, 53, 61–62, 65
   naïve, 76
   justification by, 24
Federal Theological Seminary 16
flesh (sarx), 73–74, 77
freedom
   church as sphere of (see church)
   necessitas of, 55
   of the Spirit, 32, 55
   responsible, 55, 78

friendship, x, 42, 52, 54–56
German Resistance, xi, 1, 23, 42, 44–45, 54, 80
Gnosticism, 74
Great Awakening, 19
God (see also Christ) 29, 33, 41, 46, 57, 66, 72, 76
   as Trinity, 31, 55
   desire for, 40, 75
   humanity of, 42, 79
   image of, 77–78
   incarnate, 64, 74, 79
   kingdom of, x, 12,19, 52
   love for/of, 33, 39, 46–47
   mystery of, 33–34, 67, 70
   projection of, 66
   suffering of, 39
   trust in, 2
   will of, 40, 82
   word of, 33, 48

Harlem Renaissance, 43
happiness, x, 37–42, 49, 52–53, 55–6, 82
   suffering and, 45–46, 81
heresy, 9
   apartheid as, 27, 32–33
   triumphalist, 14, 30
Holocaust, 37
Holy Spirit, 7, 32, 35–36
   creativity of, 53
   freedom of, 32, 50, 55
hubris, 52, 59–60, 68, 80
human, (see also image of God)
   agency, 71
   being, 58, 62–63, 70–71, 72–73, 78
   dignity, 78
   rights, 76
humanity, 44, 47, 52, 54, 58, 63, 65, 67, 72, 80
   crime against, 70
   affirming, 69, 70
   despisers of, 60

Index of Subjects

humanity *(continued)*
    dehumanization, 62–68
    restoration of, 64, 72
Humanism
    Bonhoeffer's, 45–6
    Renaissance, 51
    Secular, 44–45, 51

Idealism, 17
idolatry, 30, 66
immortality, 75
    digital, 71
Independents, 6–7, 18
intentional community, 79–80
International Court of Justice, 71

Jesus Christ (see also Christology), ix, 6–7, 9, 29, 32, 35, 44
    and freedom, 50
    as *cantus firmus* x, 41
    as Black, 16
    as community, 41, 52
    as Lord, 18, 29, 31–32, 44
    as prophet, 35
    as Word, 31
    existing for others, 31, 47, 52, 79
    following, 9, 11, 23, 28
    humanity of, 66–67, 79
    mind of, 20
    two-natures of, 30–31, 74
    vicarious representation, 45, 80
joy (see also happy), 40, 53
Jubilee Year, 34

Kairos Document, 5, 27–28

language
    non-religious, 48–49
    poetic, 49
    prophetic, 48–49
    soul, 73, 75–78
"Lectures on Christology" (Bonhoeffer), 30
Led into Mystery (de Gruchy), 65
Legalism, 52, 55

life, ix, 1, 39–41, 43, 47, 51–52, 54, 58, 62, 65, 85
    family, 51
    fulfilled, 79, 87
    in Christ, 79, 87
    inner, 48, 73, 76
    in prison, 85
    married, 46
    monastic, 48
    polyphony of, 41, 45–47, 57
    public, 51
    world, of the, 48, 67
lived experience, 65
Life Together (Bonhoeffer), 43
London Missionary Society, 7
love
    agape, 46
    and justice, 36, 67
    brotherly, 49, 55
    eros, 46
    of God, 33, 39, 46–47, 55
    redemptive, 2
    romantic, 49
Love Letters from Cell 92 (Bonhoeffer and von Wedemeyer), 86
Lutheran Church, 24, 35, 43, 51

machines, 59–60, 67, 69, 71, 73
    humans as, 76
Magnificat, 35
Manichaeism, 74
Mandates, 51
Maria Laach monastery, 87
marriage, 51, 55–56
medical science, 64–65, 78
Menno Simons Lectures, 21
Mennonites (see Anabaptists) 5, 18
Message to the People of South Africa, 16
metanoia (conversions) x, 67
Methodist, 7, 12, 50
mind (*nous*), 58, 69, 73–76, 78, 82
monasticism, 85

Index of Subjects

Moravian, 10
   Losungen, 85

National Socialism, 31, 38, 44
Nexus (Hariri), 79
Nicene Creed, 5, 30, 32–33, 35, 74, 79
Nonconformist
   Churches, 7–8, 11, 26
   conscience, 7

Odyssey (Homer), 66
optimism, 2
Orthodoxy, 29–30, 33–34
   Eastern, 30, 33–34
   Dissenting, 34
   Oriental, 30
orthopraxis, 33
"Outline for a Book" (Bonhoeffer), 47
Oxford Companion to Christianity, 76

pacifism, 18, 22
patriotism, 23
peace and justice, 2, 38, 80–81
   God's peace, 48
   peace-making, 23, 43, 55
Peasants' Revolt, 18
Philokalia, 81
Pilgrim Fathers, 19
philosophy
   Hellenistic, 62, 74
   moral, 40
play, 52–54
pleasure, 40, 43
Plymouth Brethren, 11
poetry, 53, 64
   Bonhoeffer's, 39–40, 49, 86
politics, 14
   global, 60
   soul of, 77
power
   grasping for, 46, 80
   imperial, 32
   papal, 38
   political, 44
   truth to, 28
   will to, 71
   worship of, 31, 52
prayer, 66, 84
   and justice, 49, 79
Presbyterian, 9, 27
Presbyterian Church of Southern Africa, 27
Program to Combat Racism, 25–26
progress, 4, 67–68
   technological, 81
prophecy, 24, 26
Protestant (see Reformation), xi, 6, 8, 13–14, 17–18, 33, 51
   Liberal, 17
Psalms, 85
psyche, (see soul), 73–75
Puritans, 14

Quakers, 6

racism, 25–26, 43, 50, 70
reason, 44, 73, 76, 85
reconciliation, xii, 70
   cheap, 28, 34
   justice, and, 70, 81
Reformation (see Protestant)
   Magisterial, 17
   Radical, 17
Reformed (see Calvinism), 17, 20, 28
responsibility, 39, 69
   free responsibility, 24, 51
   social, 42
restraint
   ministry of, 50, 80
resurrection (see immortality) 47, 74
robots/tics, 58, 63–65, 69, 71, 76–79
Roman Catholic Church, 8, 33
Rondebosch United Church, 26–27

Index of Subjects

saint/s, 38–39
salvation, 34, 64, 74
sanctification, 39
Sanctorum Communio (Bonhoeffer), 79
science (see technology), xi, 51, 62, 68, 76
Scripture Union, 11
Sea Point Congregational Church, 10
Second International Bonhoeffer Congress, 86
Second Vatican Council, 34, 75, 78
self (see soul), 73–75
  authentic, 75–76, 78
  awareness, 75
  centred, 40–42, 47
  consciousness, 76
  deception, 84
  pity, 84
  preservation, 49
  sufficient, 71
Sermon on the Mount, 18, 23, 47
Sharpeville Massacre, 15
silence, 63, 65
slavery, 11, 43, 50, 67
solidarity, x, 28, 45–46, 55
souls/s (see psyche, self)
  embodied, 73, 77, 78
  immortal, 74
  living, 72, 77
South African Council of Churches, 15
Soweto Uprising, 16, 21, 26
spirit (*pneuma*), 73, 76
Spirituals, African American, 77
Star Wars, 62
State of Emergency, 27
suffering, 2, 23, 38–39, 45, 53, 64, 82
suicide x, 38, 84

Technics and Civilization (Mumford), 67

technology (see machines, science), xi, 59, 64–65, 71, 76
  cybernetic, 60–61
  medical, 64–65, 78
The Congregational Way (de Gruchy), 6, 15
The Church Struggle in South Africa (de Gruchy), 21
The Local Church and Racial Identity (de Gruchy), 6
The Self and the Dramas of History, (Niebuhr), 75
Theology, 22
  Barth's, 12–13
  Black, 16
  Bonhoeffer's, xii, 30, 42
  Forsyth's, 6
  Kairos, 27–28
  liberal, 11, 13, 17
  life-affirming, 86
  lived, 66
  Reformed, 15, 17
"The Past" (Bonhoeffer), 49
time/s (see *kairos, Kairos Document*) ix, x, 1–3, 83–87
Tower of Babel, 59
transcendence, 68, 75
transhumanism, 68
transvaluation (see consciousness), 68
Trinity (see God), 32–33
triumphalism (see heresy)
truth, 78, 80–81

United Congregational Church of Southern Africa, 5
Union Congregational Church Cape Town, 11
Union Theological Seminary, New York, 42
United Democratic Front, 27
University of Cape Town, xii, 13–14, 26

value/s, 44–45, 68–69, 81, 118

Index of Subjects

vital balance, 61
Voluntary Act (1875), 5, 9, 50

War
  South African (Anglo-Boer), 2
  First World War, 13, 17
  Second World War, 2, 20, 38, 118

Whither South Africa (Keet), 14
wisdom, 66, 78
World Alliance for Promoting Friendship through the Churches, 55
World Council of Churches, 15, 25, 34

Index of Scripture

Leviticus
25:1–13   35

Psalm
31:15   84

Isaiah
61:1–2   35

Mark
1:14   x
12:17   8

Luke
4:16–21   35
16:31   35

John
1:14   73
10:10   41
15:13   55

Romans
10:9   32
12:1–2   82

2 Corinthians
3:17   32

Galatians
5:1   50

www.ingramcontent.com/pod-product-compliance
Lightning Source LLC
Chambersburg PA
CBHW031347160426
43196CB00007B/758

9798385261208